Yorkshire Disasters

Bomb disposal memorial, Eden Camp.

YORKSHIRE DISASTERS

A Social and Family History

Vivien Teasdale

Wharncliffe Books

By the same author:
Huddersfield Mills
Huddersfield Mill Memories
Foul Deeds & Suspicious Deaths Around Huddersfield

First published in Great Britain in 2008 by
Wharncliffe Books
An imprint of
Pen & Sword Books Ltd
47 Church Street
Barnsley
South Yorkshire
S70 2AS

ISBN: 978 184563 058 4

A CIP catalogue record for this book is available from the
British Library

Printed and bound in Great Britain
By CPI UK

Pen & Sword Books Ltd incorporates the Imprints of Pen
& Sword Aviation, Pen & Sword Maritime, Pen & Sword
Military, Wharncliffe Local History, Pen & Sword Select,
Pen & Sword Military Classics, Leo Cooper, Remember
When, Seaforth Publishing and Frontline Publishing

For a complete list of Pen & Sword titles please contact
PEN & SWORD BOOKS LIMITED
47 Church Street, Barnsley, South Yorkshire,
S70 2AS, England
E-mail: enquiries@pen-and-sword.co.uk
Website: www.pen-and-sword.co.uk

Contents

Introduction

A disaster can be described as an event that causes great loss or misfortune and Yorkshire has had its fair share of these. Some may be natural disasters but most revolve around human intervention in some way. A number of these 'disasters' first appeared as articles in *Practical Family History* but I have revised these and added to them, selecting a range of types of disasters spread throughout the county and across the years. Choices had to be made. Including the Sheffield Flood does not diminish the impact or loss incurred during the Holmfirth Flood, which took place twelve years previously. Disasters occurring in the mines, in the mills, on the railways and during the war are so numerous and the records relatively complete that it was more a question of putting the events in a hat and seeing what came out first. But with all the events, I have tried to show the human impact as well as give information that may be of use to anyone trying to trace ancestors who could have been involved in any way – an event that merely destroys property may be unfortunate but even one life lost is a disaster for someone. This book brings back memories of some lost ones and reminds us of the carelessness or even stupidity which, in many cases, caused these accidents, as well as acknowledging the bravery of the many who were involved in rescue attempts.

Deaths, and acknowledgements of sympathy, are often found in newspapers. The following notice was placed by the Handley family in the *Pontefract and Castleford Express* after the death of their daughter at Barnbow, and, for me, sums up how many of us feel in the aftermath of such disasters:

Death often comes to show
We love far better than we know;
But love in death should make us see
What love in life should always be.

Acknowledgements

As always many people have provided support and practical help in finding records of disasters. Library and archive staff are always willing to search indexes, offer suggestions for further research and advice on knotty problems such as copyright. Particular thanks to the library staff at Kirklees, Wakefield Balne Lane, Morley, Leeds Central, Hull Central, Pontefract, York Central, Huddersfield Examiner; staff at West Yorkshire Archives at Wakefield, Kirklees, Bradford and Calderdale, North Yorkshire Archives, South Yorkshire Archives at Rotherham, Barnsley, Sheffield. Help was also forthcoming from the staff at the Royal National Lifeboat Institute Museum, Whitby, who took the time to open display cupboards to allow me to photograph the contents; from Anne Batchelor who gave me valuable information and advice regarding the Barnbow incident and the Ministry of Defence for their help in finding details of the Snaith explosion. Thanks also to Brian Elliott for his support in the production of the book and to the many nameless passers-by who took the time to give me directions to obscure corners of churchyards, museums and viewpoints.

All photographs and illustrations are from the author's collection, with the exception of:
Booth factory, back cover, courtesy of *Huddersfield Daily Examiner*, 1941.
Barnsley Public Hall Victims, page 88, from *Lloyds News Supplement*.
Illustration of 'Loss of Steam Packet, Union', page 81, courtesy of Richard Hayton.
Photo of Tricomposite railway carriage, page 117, courtesy of Vintage Carriages Trust.
Maps, courtesy of Ordnance Survey.

Finally, as always, none of this would be possible without the support of family and friends, particularly my husband, my mother and sister. This book is dedicated to the memory of my father, Harold Walters, who served in the Forces during the war and afterwards for many years in the West Riding Police Force, dealing with many different disasters and providing support and sympathy to the bereaved families.

Part 1

Working Lives

1

Colne Bridge Mill Fire

Huddersfield

1818

Three miles outside Huddersfield, just off the busy Leeds Road, is an area known as Colne Bridge, which nowadays consists of little more than industrial buildings. But just over the bridge is a large pub that used to be known as the *Spinners Arms* but is now called the *Royal and Ancient*. If you go there, you might be startled to find your glass smashed or lights flickering unexpectedly. It is supposed to be haunted by the ghosts of seventeen girls who died in the nearby mill on Valentine's Day, 1818.

Royal & Ancient pub

Cotton was in demand in the early years of the nineteenth century. Mills worked every hour they could, workers often completing fourteen hour shifts, or even longer if there was an order to finish. Children too were expected to work long hours, sometimes alongside other members of their families, but they were often pauper apprentices, farmed out by the overseers to get them off local rates.

Colne Bridge Mill, owned by Thomas Atkinson, worked both day and night shifts, spinning the slivers or rovings of cotton into yarn ready for sale. Older girls worked on the spinning machines, assisted by children as young as nine, who squirmed under and around the machines keeping them clean, or ran up and down fetching and carrying whatever was needed.

Twenty-six people were working there that night, 'spinning their young lives into the yarn that enriched the mill owners' (DFE Sykes: *Huddersfield and its Vicinity*). It was dark inside the mill so when young James Thornton was sent to collect more rovings from the card room below where the girls were working at their spinning machines, he wanted to take a light with him. A glass lamp was provided specifically for the purpose of lighting the way around the mill, but perhaps ten-year-old James didn't know how to light it, or perhaps he was 'showing off' his bravery in taking a lighted candle instead. Or perhaps the overseer told him to take the candle instead of the lamp, which is the story that James later told.

A minute later, according to one of the overlookers, realising what the lad had done, the supervisor ran after him, but Thornton had already reached the card room.

The air in a cotton mill was full of cotton dust; fine bits of the fibres would stick together and form balls of cotton wool, picking up the grease from the machines. It is probable that the draught from opening the door caused the candle flame to splutter, or perhaps a piece of fluff drifted into the flame and ignited. Within seconds the skeps of cotton stored underneath the stairs were ablaze.

Thornton, in terror at what he had done, ran upstairs to shout a warning to the others, then turned and fled the building.

The card room was filled with cotton – in rovings ready for spinning, in cheeses of finished yarns and in great bales of raw material. The interior of the mill was built of wood – wooden steps, wooden floors and ceilings, and a wooden tunnel that connected the top floor with the card room, through which bundles of finished cotton could be dropped, and through which the flames were drawn rapidly upwards.

People from round about ran to help but the fire was already too far advanced. In an effort to save the girls, a ladder was put up to a small window at the furthest end of the mill, near the manager's house. It was hoped that the girls would make their way there, away from the centre of the fire, but as soon as the glass was smashed a dense column of smoke poured out of the window and that area too was soon alight. Within half an hour, nothing remained of the mill or its inhabitants but the counting house and warehouse nearby.

When the fire had died down sufficiently, a search was made but only fifteen bodies were recovered. It was presumed that the two others had been totally destroyed in the heat of the flames.

Over eighty workers lost their jobs as a consequence of the fire. The *Leeds Mercury* newspaper was glad to report that the mill, machinery and stock were all insured with the Sun and Phoenix Fire Offices. At least the mill owners would not suffer from its loss – they also owned another large woollen mill in the town.

Over the years it has been suggested that some part of the mill had, in fact, been locked and the key mislaid, which was why the girls could not escape. However, the *Leeds Intelligencer* newspaper suggested that the overlookers had managed to get the girls to the top of the stairs but some were lost when the stairs collapsed and it was presumed that the others ran back into the mill in fear. Fourteen of the bodies were found near to the window where the rescue attempt had been made, so they had obviously tried to get to safety. None of the contemporary newspaper reports suggested that any door had been locked, and in fact nine people did get out of the mill. Unfortunately the original inquest documents can no longer be found so the facts cannot be verified. However, the *Wakefield and Halifax Journal* report on the inquest told a slightly different story.

Few of the bodies could be identified but an inquest had to be held on the 'shocking remains of these poor fifteen wretches … no trace of the two remaining ones are to be found'. On the Monday after the fire, the inquest was held before James Wigglesworth, a local solicitor and landowner. The inquiry seems to have put some of the blame onto one of the overlookers, William Smith, who apparently rushed up to rescue his daughter, Mary, but once he had made sure she was safe turned his attention to 'the preservation of his master's property' rather than doing anything to save the other girls.

One of the girls actually had a miraculous escape. She had reached the top of the stairs, probably with the others who perished when the stairs collapsed. But as the stairs fell, somehow she was thrown forward and out at the open door, surviving with only a dislocated wrist and a few scratches.

This event too belies the subsequent rumours that the door was locked. It would appear that in writing about the event years later, people remembered that there had been some controversy over the role played by the overlooker and just embroidered the details.

After the inquest eleven coffins were brought into which all fifteen remains were placed, being taken in three hearses up to Kirkheaton church.

Kirkheaton Church

On the journey, the procession 'preceded by solemn music' stopped at the house of each victim and a psalm was sung there. Kirkheaton church choir, joined by others in the area especially for the occasion, sang a specially adapted anthem during the service. The girls were buried in one grave, outside the church where many had been baptised just a few years before. Three years later a stone monument was erected as a memorial to the girls, paid for by public subscription. Sarah Moody, who survived, Mary and Elizabeth were sisters, daughters of William and Rachel Moody. None of the others were related, but many came from the same villages round about and knew each other well.

Those who escaped were:

Name	Age
William Smith	60
James Sugden	40
Dolly Bolton	35
Mary Smith	20
Esther Brook	18
Mary Hay	12
Sarah Moody	11
David Sugden	10
James Thornton	10

Memorial stone for the girls

In 1802 the first ever Factory Act had been passed, to regulate the conditions of apprentices in wool and cotton mills, reducing their working hours to twelve. Partly because of this incident at Colne Bridge, which caused a national outcry, the government was forced to bring in a further law regulating the length of hours employees could be expected to work. Children under nine could not be employed and those under sixteen could work a maximum of seventy-two hours a week, with an hour and a half per day for meal breaks.

Sources:
Leeds Intelligencer 1818
Wakefield and Halifax Journal 1818
Huddersfield Weekly Examiner 1818

2

Hembrigg Mill Explosion

Morley, Leeds

1863

On Saturday 27 June 1863, the people of Morley set off to work as usual. James Marshall was delivering newspapers to his father's customers around the area, but most were heading into the local mills, called by the strident buzzers warning them to get to work on time. The workers started at six in the morning and worked for two and a half hours before getting half an hour for their breakfast. Some went home for this, but many others stayed around the mill or sat out in the sunshine in the mill yard. Business was booming in the area and most of the mills were working at full capacity, adding more machines and requiring more and more power to meet their orders.

Hembrigg Mill was a five-storey building at the west end of the village, near the viaduct of the Leeds, Bradford and Halifax railway and about 150 yards from the station. It was built around 1861, the main building being 51 yards long and 18 yards wide. Part of the lower storey was used as a warehouse whilst the rest housed the engine that provided power throughout the mill. Although it was owned by Henry Hirst, a cloth manufacturer, of Morley, he did not work in the mill but rented rooms out to four other firms – Hirst Bros (his sons); Isaac Bradley; Nathaniel Bradley; and John Hirst. The engine seemed to be small to do the work, not quite being up to the power expected by the tenants, but it had to do, Mr Hirst was preparing to 'lay down' an upright beam engine of sixty-horse power. Messrs Sands and Walker had received an order for it, and Mr Hirst was having a detached brick building erected about 20 yards from but almost directly opposite the gable end of the mill and flues had been built to join up with the chimney.

The mill chimney, on the south-east of the main building and close to a row of brick built cottages, was 36 yards high, built of brick and almost cylindrical. The existing engine, which drove the machinery within the building, was in a two-storey building at the gable end of the mill and the room above the boiler was used as a drying-house, having a perforated iron floor of about half an inch in thickness. All around the mill were cottages and other mills.

The engine tenter, David Thackrah, stayed behind as usual, oiling and checking the machinery that he could not reach when the giant boiler and steam engine were running. At nine o'clock the buzzer would sound to bring everyone back to work but many were already drifting in when, at eight-fifty, there was a massive explosion at the end of the factory and the engine house disintegrated in a roar and crash of falling iron, stone and wood. The explosion was heard all over Morley and the surrounding neighbourhood. Almost immediately people rushed to the place to begin the search for survivors.

On the road, not far from the mill, they first discovered the body of a man, dreadfully disfigured. He was Nathaniel Dickinson, a beamer, who had been struck by a brick on his chest whilst returning to the mill after breakfast. His body was quickly taken to his home in Hollow. Then, about 50 yards from the mill, they found the body of ten-year-old James Marshall, one of eight children of Joseph Marshall who was a weaver and newsagent from Hunger Hill, in Morley. The lad had been taking newspapers to customers when struck by a piece of iron. Though he was taken home he died after seven hours of extreme agony.

Little hope was held out for others actually in the mill at the time. The bodies of Thackrah and William Pilkington, a sixty-seven-year-old wool scourer were found 30 yards away. They had both been sitting in front of the boiler when it exploded, and both had been decapitated by the blast. Their bodies too were taken home, as was the corpse of Emma Carr (or Foster) the fifteen-year-old daughter of George Carr of Gillroyd.

William Champion of Sheffield suffered a fractured skull, from which he died instantly, but John Varley, a young overlooker, who suffered the same injury, was taken to Leeds Infirmary in the hope that something could be done for him. John Wilson, a seventeen-year-old who was just returning to work after his breakfast, was also taken to Leeds.

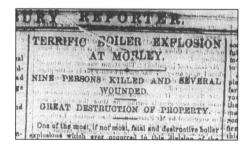

Others, such as fifty-four-year-old Thomas Smith and Margaret Kaye, a fourteen-year-old piecer who suffered chest injuries and broken arm, were pulled out injured and taken home, only to die later on that day.

Headline, Dewsbury Reporter

A medical 'team' was soon in action. Two local doctors – Mr Hirst and Mr Ellis, quickly arrived, as did Mr King from the Leeds Infirmary. Surprisingly, some people were found alive and the doctors were able to provided immediate help.

Charlotte Brigg, a weaver, had been outside the mill door and was struck on the back of the head by debris, though her sister, Ann, aged just ten, who had been taking Charlotte's breakfast to her, was severely injured. Seventeen-year-old William Bentley was much luckier. He was merely bruised and was sent home, as was Luke Lowry, an Irish labourer. Henry Hirst junior, a son of the mill owner, was both bruised and scalded from the steam but was not seriously injured. Others named included Lucy Lupton, a weaver, David Matthews and two children – a girl named Ward and a boy named England.

The cottage dwellers round about had some narrow escapes, though many of the buildings and furniture in the cottages were badly damaged. One piece of the mill fell on a cottage opposite the gable end of the mill, occupied by Joseph Charlesworth, a shoemaker. He and one child were in the workroom, whilst his wife, Rachel, her brother and two children were in the sitting room. A tube crashed through the roof and knocked down the outer wall, covering them with debris. People round about rescued Rachel and her brother, then found her thirteen-year-old daughter, Ann, who had some cuts. The next cottage was occupied by Robert Brydon, who was in the cottage at the time. Though much damage was done, no one was injured as was the case next door where Edwin Longbottom, a stonemason, lived with his wife and little boy.

Almost immediately a meeting was called at the *White Horse Inn* for that evening chaired by William S King, the surgeon who had done so much to help the injured and a relief fund was set up. The committee consisted of William King, chairman, Robert Nevin, Joseph Mortimer, Charles Wickner, George Jowett, Thomas Marshall, Thomas Briggs, James Peel, Joseph Rhodes, Samuel Schofield, Joseph Schofield, Humphrey Bradley, William Scarth, John Driver, Edward Stockwell, William Baines, Thomas Barrows, John Appleyard, Fred Tesseyman, Samuel Scott and John Greenwood. Knowing the attraction such an event would have on the local populace, they decided that they would each take turns:

'... to carry a box round amongst the strangers and visitors to the scene of the calamity and solicit from them subscriptions towards the relief fund. Thomas Briggs being appointed treasurer. The sum realised up to Sunday night by the above means was £68 and the collections made on Monday brought the amount up to near £100.'

White Horse Inn, Morley

On Monday morning, 29 June, the inquest into the deaths of seven people: Nathaniel Dickinson, William Pilkington, Thomas Smith, James Marshall, Emma Foster (Carr), David Thackrah and William Champion, was opened at the *Albion Hotel*, Townend, Morley, close to the scene of the catastrophe, before E Jewison, coroner, and a jury consisting of: Joseph Rhodes, foreman, William Dixon, John Jackson, James Smith, Henry Webster, Joseph Milner, Abraham Barker, William Marshall, Joseph Snowden, John Clough, Samuel Naylor, William Middlebrook, Jonathan Robinson and John Hirst.

The coroner then announced that he had been spoken to by 'a gentleman' from Huddersfield who wished to look at the boiler. He was believed to be an engineer, but the jury wanted to know if he represented anyone in particular and could be biased. They wanted to find someone who would not be biased but could make a clear report on the matter. The police inspector said he too had been approached by another man who said he represented the Steam Boiler Company and had been sent by Mr Hirst. Neither had been allowed to look at the ruins or the mangled boiler.

Albion Hotel, Morley

Unfortunately, the coroner didn't know of any government inspector of boilers, but it was obvious they did need to ascertain the quality of the iron used in the boiler. Joseph Hopkinson, who had first approached the coroner to inspect the boiler, then stated that he did not represent anyone, was not from an insurance company but had inspected, on behalf of the coroner, the boilers in explosions at Learoyd's and at Kaye's in Huddersfield and another at Hargreave's at Accrington. (The *Dewsbury Reporter* newspaper later went on to comment that there had been more than nine boiler explosions in the area over the past month, and suggested that it was time something was done about it). Hopkinson said that he had read a paper to the British Association on steam boilers and was preparing another one for the next meeting. He was at the inquest 'entirely on his own bottom' and would give a fair and honest account. The jury then agreed and authorised him to go and prepare a statement for them whilst they went off to view the bodies and inspect the ruins.

Each of the seven was then formally identified by their next of kin, so that the bodies could be released for burial.

Henry Hirst, the mill owner, was then questioned, but also told that he did not have to say anything if he felt it would incriminate himself. He declared that he had nothing to fear, though he admitted that the fireman and carrier were in his direct employ, whereas the other people killed had all, except James Marshall, been employed by his tenants. He simply provided the power for the mill:

'I reside at Morley and have been a cloth manufacturer. I am the owner of Hembrigg Mill where the boiler burst on Saturday last. It was what we call a fire-box or Cornish boiler, of forty horse power and was made by Israel Newton of Farnley Moor Edge. The inside (the flues) were of the Low Moor best iron. I don't know what sort of iron the outside was nor where it came from but the plates were seven-sixteenths of an inch thick and those of the flues half an inch. It was two and a half years since the boiler was first made use of though it was put up two years since last Christmas. The price I paid for the boiler was £15 10 shillings per ton and the amount I paid for it altogether was £216. The inspector, who came from Manchester, for the company with which I had insured the boiler said to me that it would bear 70lb pressure per inch and that it might be worked at 80lb per inch with safety. I said "that will do then, I only want to work it at 40lb". I insured the boiler, not to the full amount, but for £100 only with the Manchester Steam Boiler Insurance Company about a year ago, principally for the sake of inspection and their inspector has been three times to look at and examine it since. I believe he went inside it last time he came about six weeks since and that was the time he told me what pressure it might be worked. When the inspector first called he said to me "I shall put this boiler down as first class but there are some that I would not have at all – this is the best boiler I have seen anywhere in this neighbourhood."

The coroner made the comment: 'I should think there can be no doubt about that,' which suggests that he had already decided there was no case to answer, but Hirst continued:

'I don't pay a high premium for insurance it is not more than £1 per year. The second time the inspector came he advised me to have the lever on the escape valve lengthened and left the length with the fireman, who got it done by my order. This was done so that the steam would blow off at 40lb pressure. The fireman – David Thackrah – than whom a more cautious man could exist – did not do it himself but gave it his brother in the town to do. The first I heard the steam blow off the lever had not been lengthened

according to the measurements left by the inspector … I then found by the gauge that the pressure was at 40 and have since that time frequently heard it blowing off when it has got to 40. The fireman could see the gauge when he was feeding as it was just beside him when he was at that job. I have never instructed the fireman to put a larger or more weights on the lever for we never had any occasion to put on a higher pressure. We ran at 37 to 40lb and if we got to 40 the engine went rather too fast for the looms and the weavers stopped work and ran to the fireman who then reduced the speed. When it got to 40 the steam blew off and it had to be decreased before the looms could resume working. The engine was a condenser but I cannot say the exact power though it was made nominally as a 16-horse by Messrs Sands and Walker of Heckmondwike.'

Mr Hopkinson interrupted to ask what the diameter of the cylinder was, and, on being told 22 inches, he calculated that it would actually be 20-horse power nominally.

When Hirst had finished, Hopkinson, a civil engineer from Huddersfield, took the stand. He had examined the exploded boiler at Hembrigg Mill that morning and now produced the safety valve. He demonstrated that the spindle would not move either up or down and the valve itself was fast instead of being able to be opened or shut. He had found it in that state and while the lever was very much bent by the explosion, he also explained to the jury that the lever was also twisted by the weight suspended on it, which had pressed it to one side, a position which he believed could not have been produced by the strain upon it from the accident. The lever was not in a position to act freely in the slot on account of the twist and there was also another defect as the top of the spindle was flat, a fault which had often been pointed out before. The flatness would cause the spindle to press against the side of the hole in which it should have worked, though the fulcrum ought to be exactly in the middle as it would have been if the spindle had been pointed.

He could not say what caused the spindle to be fast as he had not taken the bonnet off the valve-box before he had shown it to the jury and checked that it was all right to remove the bonnet. This was agreed to, the valve was loosened and withdrawn by one of the jurymen, who had to struggle to wrench it open. Mr Hopkinson then examined the spindle and valve and pointed out that the valve had never been properly seated and from this cause the steam would blow off some even when the pressure was at 20lbs, and the valve itself with working in a slanting position would be liable to get stuck as had been found to be the case. It might have been in that condition without the knowledge of the engineman, but he ought not to have been ignorant of the friction of the twisted lever against the two edges of the slot in which it worked. The defect in the lever and valve was one cause of the explosion and defects in some parts of the boiler second.

He described his findings on the boiler:

'It appeared to be made of Staffordshire iron. He could not find any Low Moor mark but in the flues he found a mark TB and a crown which meant Thorncroft's best plate Staffordshire iron. It was an average quality, the shell was barely half-an-inch thick and the flue seven to ten pounds weight but he might add that as regards Mr Hirsts's statement as to the cost of iron plates, the price of Low Moor best plate was £21 per ton and on boilers complete of that iron £28, not £15 10 shillings. He'd attributed the cause of the explosion in the first instance to over-pressure from the safety valves having been rendered inoperative by defects in its construction and he believed the steam would not blow off until it sustained 50lbs pressure per inches instead of 40lbs in consequence of the lengthening. At least a foot had been added, and twistings, with its consequent friction, of the lever making no allowance at all for the valve being wrongly seated and fast. In the next place the explosion was caused by a sort of defect in the staying of the boiler ends by gusset stays – the proper mode being in his opinion to put bolts from end to end. The pressure at the time must have been far higher than 70lbs to produce such disastrous results.'

Again, the coroner put in his little comment: 'Yes, or 80lbs either for the power has been tremendous, it has been more like an eruption of Mount Etna or Vesuvius than anything else.'

Hopkinson continued that he did not see any traces of scarcity of water. Had this been the case the scale would have been taken off the plates, nor could he see anything that would lay blame on the engine tenter. In fact, he felt that the insurance inspector should have known of the defects in the valve if he had examined it as he ought to have done.

This provoked the coroner to comment: 'This insurance inspector seems to have lulled them [Messrs Hirst] into a false sense of security – he has misled them. Mr Hirst said the lever had been lengthened 'precisely as the inspector told them to.' The coroner then stated that he felt there was no criminal responsibility on either the owner or the engine tenter, but that too often the only qualification required of an engine tenter was that they be 'steady' and 'do their best', the best, too frequently, being to accept low wages. Mr Hirst immediately explained that he paid Thackrah 24 shillings per week. Jewison 'expressed his satisfaction' that this was a fair wage and Mr Hirst was acquitted of any blame in that respect.

The jury retired to decide their verdict but at this point, Mr A B Longridge from Manchester, the chief engineer of the Steam Boiler Insurance Company arrived. He apologised for his lateness and there was some discussion as to whether he would be allowed to give evidence. Finally he spoke to the coroner, his comments being passed to the jury:

'The boiler was examined by one of the company's inspectors some time in the month of May and after that inspection a written report was sent from the office to Mr Hirst to the effect that the safety valve was overloaded and out of order. The maximum pressure that the boiler was to work was 40lbs per inch as stated in the policy but with the extra weights attached to the lever when the inspection was last made it was loaded beyond that pressure and that caused the report to be sent.'

Jewison argued that this was not evidence, '... you are only stating what another person reported'.

'But,' said Longridge, 'a written report was sent to Mr Hirst and he can produce it.'

'Did you send it?'

'No, but I saw the copy and know it was sent from the office.'

Mr Hirst was then sent for and his evidence read over to Mr Longridge, who denied giving any orders for the lengthening of the lever, but admitted telling Mr Hirst that the boiler might be worked at 60lb pressure if the engine had been a larger one and he wrote the report when the boiler was insured.

Mr Hirst could not say Mr Longridge was the inspector who had left the calculations for the lengthening with the fireman, as he did not see him and said distinctly that no written report as mentioned by Mr Longridge had been received by him – he had never seen one.

The jury was then left to consider its verdict, which, not surprisingly was 'that the deceased parties were accidentally killed by the explosion of a boiler – caused by the safety valve getting fast by some means unknown'. The comment from the local newspaper was that:

'Great dissatisfaction exists in Morley at the slovenly manner in which the enquiry has been conducted and the speedy manner in which it was closed.'

However, John Varley and John Wilson, who had been taken to Leeds Infirmary, had since died and Leeds coroner, Mr Blackburn, held a further inquest at the Town Hall. He delved into the question of the boiler more thoroughly, questioning Nathanial Pearson, a cloth manufacturer occupying part of Hembrigg Mill and employer of the late John Wilson. He had not been aware of the boiler being defective but thought the engine was not sufficiently powerful for the mill, though he had not heard anyone say the boiler was running at too much pressure.

The coroner also found out that Thackrah, the engine tenter, had actually left the employ of Mr Hirst the previous year and had only recently returned.

Blackburn wanted to know why Thackrah had left his employment. Mr Hirst denied that it was anything to do with safety and said that Thackrah had returned within a week but another witness, David Bradley, said the reason Thackrah left the position was that he felt he 'was always in danger'. When the replacement had 'trashed' the engine, Hirst got Thackrah to go back promising to work only half the mill at a time to ease the pressure. They worked half the mill in the daytime and half at night and gradually put on more pressure until they got back to the old situation of working all the mill at once. He had heard that Thackrah was going to leave on Saturday.

Pearson then corroborated the agreement to work only half the mill at a time to avoid breakages, but in his opinion the valves had been out of order and it had not been known for more than a week what pressure the boiler was working at. In passing the boiler room lately he had noticed an intense heat, like that of a drying room.

Benjamin Hirst then said he did not know why Thackrah had left. When he returned, the mill had run half at a time but only for a few days to see that the engine was all right.

John Gregson, an overlooker, spoke about his confidence in Thackrah's work. He had never heard him say the boiler was worked at too high a pressure. He used to stay in the mill whilst the others were having breakfast to check and oil the parts he couldn't get to when the engine was running. William Bentley, a willier and fettler, told how he was in the new boiler house at the time of explosion with Tom Smith (who died later) and a man called Sheffield who was killed on the spot. When he had returned from home after having breakfast, Thackrah was in the firing place putting coal on the fire.

Next, Israel Newton, a boilermaker of Farnley Moor Top, who had made the boiler that burst, was asked about its construction. It was 40-horse power and new when sold, he said. It was built on the Cornish principle with two flues at £15 10s per ton made of iron from Low Moor works. Mr Brown of Leeds supplied the plates, though he was not a maker of iron. Newton thought the boiler would work safely at 40-50lbs pressure, though it had not been tested. The boiler had been repaired after fifteen months as it had been damaged through shortage of water. It had also been repaired about five months ago, when the outer plate split. He attributed this to high pressure, but admitted under questioning that it could have been from poor quality iron. He pointed out that the insurance company had said the iron was good quality. If only one place had shown damage it might have been put down to poor quality but as it leaked in other places too he felt this proved that the engine was worked at too high a pressure. He had received no complaints since the last repair. Newton agreed that it could be over pressure accidentally, but said: 'I examined the boiler and cannot find that it was short of water.' He was reminded that Gregson had looked at the gauge just before he stopped for breakfast and it read 38lbs, but as it burst half an hour after that, and Newton stated that the pressure could rise very quickly, though he admitted that then he would have expected to see or hear the steam blowing off. He also said that he had told Mr Hirst after the last repair that the pressure was too high.

The Leeds inquiry also called in Mr Brown, the iron merchant who had supplied the plates. He insisted that he didn't test the plates as the purchaser could come and select the plates they required and it was up to them to select the right ones for the job. 'I'm not responsible for what sort are selected,' he said.

Harriett Thackrah, the engine tenter's widow, described how he had first gone to Hembrigg Mill nearly two years previously, left briefly to go to another mill, then returned to Hembrigg where he had always been happy, and never expressed any fear of the boiler or engine exploding. He had called it a 'good little engine'.

Various manufacturers who rented part of the mill were called and all agreed that Thackrah had never complained about the engine. The agreement to run at 'half weight' had been temporary just to check the engine, but Joseph Walker who had made the engine insisted that it was perfectly safe to run at full pressure.

However, the Leeds coroner had commissioned his own engineer, J Hetherington of Leeds, to investigate and he stated that the plates had overheated due to lack of water, explaining that this was caused by having a safety valve which was 'too small to discharge the steam generated without throwing a larger amount of pressure upon the boiler than what is indicated by the lever and weights'. He estimated that the pressure at explosion would have been nearer 60lb, not 40. He had also examined the screw feed valve and the check valve, both of which were jammed up with ash and grit. He pointed out that whilst the engine was running this would not have caused much problem but when it was 'set down' for breakfast:

> *'The pressure of steam forced the water out of the boiler and through the check valve till it got down below the level of the flue.'*

The steam would then get into contact with the fire and become superheated, causing pressure to build up. He also pointed out that the boiler was not fully horizontal therefore when the water was low the end of the tube nearest the firing place would get burned.

He recommended that all boilers should be fitted with two safety valves and that they should be of the correct size for the boiler.

The jury then considered their verdict, finally agreeing with the Morley jury, and brought in 'accidental death', though they added the recommendation of two safety valves being fitted as suggested by Hetherington.

Later, the funds raised were distributed amongst the victims or their families. Many received small sums, such as Mrs Pilkington, Joe Wilson, Martha Dickinson, George Carr, Joseph Marshall and Joseph Charlesworth (for damage to his furniture) who received £5 each. Paul Champion of Sheffield had £4 presented to him and the overseers provided him with a coffin for the interment of his son, William. William Lupton received 30 shillings from the committee and William Stanhope £2 to defray some of the cost of repairing his furniture.

Sources:
Dewsbury Reporter 1863
Huddersfield Daily Examiner 1863

3

Fireworks Explosion

Barnsley

1868

On the north-east side of Doncaster Road, midway between the Wesleyan school and the cemetery, Waltham Road, a new thoroughfare running between Sheffield and Doncaster Road had recently been made, a little to the south of Taylor's Row. Some brick houses stood at one end of the street and at the other there was a plot of land, separated from the road by a low stone wall.

Close to the road, in the centre of the plot of land but hidden from view by the stone wall, was a small detached building with one window. It was the only building actually licensed for making fireworks, but in reality, this was simply the magazine where the gunpowder was kept. Another building, roughly constructed of wood and brick, and divided into four sheds, ran close to and parallel with the road and this was where Norris's Fireworks were really manufactured.

Norris was a hairdresser, watchmaker and jeweller as well as manufacturer of fireworks so he didn't attend the works every day. He also had three of his employees living with him – Mary Ann Evans, and her brother, Richard, who were orphans born in London and brought to Barnsley by a Mr Harrison. They lived with Mr Norris along with his assistant, Alfred Banks, who was also a hairdresser but went to the factory sometimes to supervise and work on the fireworks. Over thirty people were employed by Norris, mostly boys and girls from age nine upwards but on Tuesday 6 October many had worked late into the evening and so on the morning of Wednesday 7 October 1868 only eighteen people were in the buildings.

Alfred Banks later explained the organisation of the work and the making up of the composition, used to fill the fireworks, which consisted of nitre sulphur and charcoal and was highly combustible:

'W E Bywater and Mr Norris used to make the composition in the mixing shed – a building 8 or 10 yards away from the manufactory. After the

*composition was mixed in an earthenware pan it was fetched by the women
and children in empty powder barrels and taken into sheds one and two
where the bases were filled and finished. The foreman, Bywater, generally
worked in number two. There was an oven in the cracked grate of number
one. We used metal rammers. The composition was got out of the barrels by
iron or pewter funnels. A box about a foot square and about four to six inches
deep was kept in number one and gun powder (meal or grain) was put in it.
The girls used to make crackers in number four. My usual occupation there
was making Roman candles in number three.'*

At five minutes to seven in the morning, Norris and Banks arrived at work.
Walking through Shed 1 where Richard Evans, Jane Hawker, Tommy
Carroll, Tommy Siddons, Joe Siddons and Sarah Ann Downing, were
already hard at work, Norris headed into Shed 2, passing Edward Day who
had just started work and asking after the pig that had strayed into the
factory the previous night. Between them all they had caught it and put it
in the coal shed until its owner could be found and it was still there. Banks
went into Shed 4, where, a short while later Mrs Cooper, who supervised
the girls in Shed 4, came in. In a box lid, she had about a pound weight of
composition. That morning she complained that the composition would
not fill because it was damp but in Shed 2 there was a stove, railed round
with iron bars about five feet high and iron bars all round the top for the
purpose of putting the tins of composition on and, she said, she 'would
take it and put it over the fire if she blew the place up'.

Banks thought she was joking and continued with his work but a few
minutes later Lizzie Hewitt, who was also working in the shed, heard a
cracker explode and hurriedly closed the shed door to prevent an accident.
More crackers went off and she shouted for Alfred. They saw more fire
crackers exploding in all directions and ran quickly towards Measbrough
Dyke and crossed the Doncaster Road out of the way.

In Shed 2 Bywater and Norris suddenly smelled sulphur and looked
round. They rushed towards the stove and tried to knock the tin off but they
were too late. Bywater's later statement to the police finished the story:

*'When I next found myself I was blown into the windowsill and the windows
were out. After that I was blown out of the building into the garden. I then
found my clothing was on fire. I rolled myself on the ground and called for
help. Some person came and put me on a board and brought me home. I have
no feeling in my hands, I cannot write ...'*

Bywater was later found to have a broken back as well as horrific burns and
died the following day.

Sheds 1 and 2 were quickly engulfed in flames, fireworks exploding and fizzing all around. Day, who had been standing near the door, was thrown against the boxes, cutting his head open but he was still able to run from the building. Richard Evans and one of the little boys ran out screaming, their clothes on fire and people working in the area raced to help. Some of the bodies were dragged out and eventually taken to the nearby *Union Inn*.

John Butler, of Waltham Street, a cabinet maker, gave a particularly harrowing account. He had heard a rumbling and then the explosion. Realizing what had happened he ran to the factory and found Thomas Carroll, a young lad of thirteen, on the wall near the footpath, which was covered with the wall of the building which had blown outwards in one piece. Thomas' father, Peter, arrived and the two men helped the lad out of the building. Peter took his son, who was badly burned, home whilst Butler pulled Joseph John Siddons out of Shed 1 and continued:

'A piece of stick was on the road. I took it up and held it out to a little boy named Watson. He took hold of it but the skin came off his hands and he fell backward into the burning ruins.'

Later, water was thrown in and the body recovered. Butler continued helping others, pulling a girl out of the building.

Norris had run out of the building, his clothes on fire. Mrs Horbury lived opposite the factory and saw Norris coming, shouting: 'I'm all on fire!' Two colliers ran up and they helped her pull his clothes off. She then wrapped him up in two blankets and took him into her house, until he could be taken to his own home.

James Kaye, a joiner and builder in Sheffield Road, came as soon as he heard the explosion, seeing people in flames and helping cut clothes off the burning employees. Mrs Cooper was lying dead in the far corner of number two shed near the stove, with Sarah Hinchliffe a yard or two away. Kaye went to Horbury's to see Norris and ask how many were in buildings. Norris replied that there were only three or four but when Kaye pointed out that this could not be true as more had already been got out, Norris simply said: 'Well, don't tease me.'

Alfred Banks also went to see Norris at Horbury's house, telling him what Mrs Cooper had said to him about putting the tin on the stove. Norris' reaction was to tell him to 'hold your noise' but later Norris seemed very keen to pass on the story to the 'druggist' or pharmacist, Joseph Garwood Johnson, who went to visit Norris in his house in Sheffield Road. Johnson told the inquest that Norris 'several times said: "It's a bad job Mrs Cooper doing as she did."'

Sixteen or seventeen other youngsters employed in the factory escaped with varying degrees of burns but the final total left eleven dead.

Nothing in the form of a building remained. The site was just a confused mass of machinery and timber, with massive quantities of exploded squibs, crackers and other kinds of fireworks.

The magazine, which fortunately was a considerable distance from the sheds, was not touched; otherwise the consequences would have been even more serious since it contained not just the gunpowder but all the finished fireworks as well.

Those who died were:

Maria Cooper, thirty-five, wife of James Cooper, a colliery hurrier. Maria had previously been employed in a fireworks factory in Birmingham so she should have known what she was doing.

William Elliott Bywater, shed foreman

Mary Ann Evans and Richard Evans, brother and sister. Both of these and W E Bywater were identified by Ann, wife of William Banks, a linen weaver. Bywater was their son-in-law.

Henry Howarth, twelve, son of John Howarth, a shoemaker, originally from Bacup in Lancashire.

John Edward Watson, eleven, who had only started work at the factory the previous Monday. He was the son of John Watson, a joiner.

Jane Hawker, fourteen, daughter of Daniel Hawker, a labourer. Jane had been working for Norris for two years.

Sarah Ann Downing, twelve, daughter of Hannah Lodge and her first husband, George Downing. Hannah told the inquest jury that: 'When I saw her at the workhouse she said "Do Mother lift me up, I shall soon be with my father."'

George Norris, owner of the factory.

Harriet Ann Hinchliff (or Larkin), thirteen, who had been taken to the workhouse and died there. She was the daughter of Edmund Hinchliff, mechanic, deceased. She had lived with Rebecca and Timothy Larkin, her aunt and uncle, by whose name she was generally known. Larkin was on his deathbed at the time of the explosion and died on the Thursday just before his niece.

George Yates, nine, son of William Yates, a coal miner. George had worked for Norris for only two weeks prior to the accident.

A short inquest was held initially to identify the bodies in the various places to which they had been taken, then an inquest before a jury consisting of Mr Ostcliffe, foreman, Mr Chamberlain, John Braime, Edwin A Schofield, S Merryweather, A Badger, F Johnson, J Lowrance, Joseph Woodruff, J Chipchase, J Hornby senior, George Brown, John Wilcock, William Sykes, W G Horsfield was held in the Court House in Barnsley to confirm the cause of death and apportion blame. After hearing all the witnesses describing what had happened, the rescues that had taken place and the dismal tales of blackened bodies being brought forth, the jury retired to consider its verdict:

'We are of the opinion that M Cooper, G Norris, W E Bywater and the others came to their deaths by way of an explosion of fireworks at Barnsley on Wednesday 7 October 1868 and we are likewise of the opinion that the direct cause was the recklessness of Maria Cooper in placing a tin of composition on the stove whereby it exploded. We consequently return a verdict of manslaughter against Maria Cooper as to all the parties except herself. We are likewise of the opinion that children of such tender age ought not to be employed in such dangerous occupations and that the jury further say that there appears to have been no proper regulation in conducting the works and that the sheds were unfit for carrying on such business.'

The local newspaper, the *Barnsley Chronicle,* had some comments to make on this. Whilst they agreed that Maria Cooper was ultimately to blame they insisted the accident would not have happened if things had been run correctly, been properly supervised and the building constructed of more

Entrance way to Barnsley Cemetery

substantial materials. They made stinging criticism of the magistrates who had granted a licence and suggested that a proper inspection of the property should have been carried out first when it would have been obvious that it should never have had a licence for fireworks at all.

They went on to say that such a business should be carried out:

> '*at a safe distance from human habitation, in fireproof buildings specially adapted for the purpose and under the most stringent regulations framed in the interests of the workers. As to the workers themselves, it is also highly necessary that there should be restrictions as to age, experience and general capability.*'

The newspaper was equally scathing of the employment of young children, stating that whilst workers with experience would exercise caution, it was unlikely from children of nine or ten:

> '*How a parent could allow such things is incomprehensible – for two shillings a week!*'

The victims were buried in the local cemetery, the funerals paid for by Norris' representatives.

Source:
Barnsley Chronicle 1868

4

Collapse of Newland Mill Chimney

Bowling, Bradford

1882

Most people now realise that Victorian mills were dangerous places. The huge machinery had few guards, children crawled inside, under and over them to ensure that the looms operated non-stop. Fluff from the raw materials was everywhere; liable to catch fire anytime a bit of grit caused a spark to fly out from the machines. Boilers burst with seeming regularity, and on 21 June 1861 a boiler had exploded at the dye works of Messrs Ripley and Son, at Bowling, Bradford, causing great destruction of property, and the death of sixty-four-year-old William Rouse, and serious injury to Isaac Brook. The boiler was torn from its seat, blown in two, lengthwise, and the centre portion, weighing nearly four tons, was tossed high into the air, rolled up like sheet lead, and carried a distance of 30 yards. The cause of the accident was put down to the plate becoming so thin by corrosion that it could not bear the pressure used.

Unfortunately, fire, disease and explosion were not the only hazards. Mills were usually massive buildings of local stone or brick, the engine houses required tall chimneys that belched out smoke and both required good foundations. Good foundations were expensive.

In 1862 Sir Henry Ripley commissioned Messrs John Moulson & Sons to build an 80 yards high chimney for his mill in Bradford. The cost was agreed at £942 5s 10d. They had decided to build the chimney over an old coal shaft, which was filled with concrete to form a central pillar for the chimney. Recommendations by the local clerk of the works to have either dressed stone inside the chimney or solid brickwork were ignored. Instead there was a brick lining with stone facing and 'backing' of loose rubble between the two. However, Sir Henry, in common with many other factory owners, didn't just want a working chimney. Many industrial buildings of the time were designed to look like cathedrals, country houses or Italian villas with elaborate doorways, ornate windows and rooftops. Almost as soon as the work on the mill started, it was stopped whilst new designs were produced to make the chimney more ornate. Unfortunately, in this case, the extra work weakened the chimney and a definite tilt became obvious, with a bulge in the brickwork at one side and corresponding hollow on the other. To rectify this, one course of stones, 70 yards up the chimney, was cut out and wedges put in to make it 'as nearly perpendicular as possible'. Finally it was finished, standing proudly in the centre of the mill complex that covered the whole area between Springmill Street and Upper Castle Street. Sections of the building were rented out to various firms in the area, including A Haley & Co, W H Greenwood & Co and J Horsfall & Co.

However, over the next twenty years, repairs had to be carried out regularly to bolster up the chimney, until in 1882 cracks in the wall developed into bulges. On 20 December Mr Francis Haley, the agent and manager of the mill, wrote to Henry Ripley jnr to complain of the state of the chimney, stating that Mr Humphreys the builder at the mill 'is of the opinion that the damaged portion which is four or five yards in length, will be forced out before the end of the week'. He was told that preventing people walking near it was an adequate safety measure but no actual work was authorised. To look inside the chimney and see the full extent of the problem would have meant allowing it to cool down. That would have meant stopping work and the owners would not allow it.

Then some of the outer casing fell off and, on 28 December, after an exceptionally windy night, the whole chimney fell directly onto the mill, destroying many of the buildings and killing fifty-four people. The only thing to be thankful for was that it had not fallen a few minutes earlier. It was eight o'clock in the morning and most of the mill had just stopped work for breakfast. One comment made at the time was that it was 'not to be wondered at that the chimney fell, but the wonder is that the structure stood so long as it did'.

It took three days to recover all the bodies, many of them child workers, brought out at considerable risk to those working at the site. Matthew Laycock, who had come up from Surrey more than twenty years earlier and been appointed the first sergeant at the local police station, was later decorated for his bravery at this incident. He went on to serve Bradford until 1890 when he retired.

The inquest began on 9 January and the jury, consisting of the following persons, sworn in: John Beanland, builder; John R Cordingley, iron merchant; B Dixon, plasterer; J Perkins, iron founder; David Sowden, machinist; all of Ashgrove. Thomas Waterhouse, innkeeper, Little Horton Lane; Charles William Marchbank, innkeeper, Bridge Street; Robert Roper, quarry owner, Manningham; Samuel Ryder, plumber, Northgate; G T Cheetham, coach builder, Howard Street; S O Bailey, lithographer, Victor Road; George Walker, outfitter, St Paul's Road; Henry Wright, tobacconist, Market Street; Robert

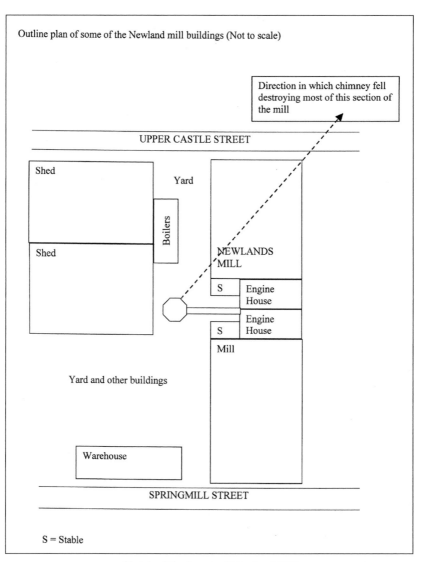

Outline plan of some of the Newland mill buildings (Not to scale)

Direction in which chimney fell destroying most of this section of the mill

UPPER CASTLE STREET

Shed

Yard

Boilers

Shed

NEWLANDS MILL

S | Engine House

Engine House
S

Mill

Yard and other buildings

Warehouse

SPRINGMILL STREET

S = Stable

Sketch of the layout of Newland Mill

Walsh, draper, Manchester Road.

One reporter wrote that 'a painfully pathetic incident was narrated by one of the witnesses', a young widow named Sarah Hancock, whose husband, John, a stone mason from Derbyshire, had recently died, leaving her with two small daughters, Margaret and Annie, and a thirteen-year-old son, James Henry. She said that as he was leaving, just before six am to go to work at the mill where he was employed as a doffer, James had said to her: 'Don't let me go this morning, someone will be killed at that place before breakfast time.' His mother had replied: 'It's my rent week this week and thou must go.'

When James stated that he'd seen the chimney move in the wind, she continued: 'The masters know better than such as ye. They will never put you in danger'.

The newspaper commented: 'We trust that the persons responsible for his safety will not go unpunished.'

Despite evidence that the owners had known of the dangerous state of the chimney, a verdict of accidental death was found.

James Henderson was the father of two of the girls killed in the accident and in 1884 he took Sir Edward Ripley, Ripley's brothers and a Mr Taylor to court. The case appeared before Justice Manisty and jury at Leeds summer assizes. Henderson was a wool comber working for Greenwoods, a firm which rented part of Ripley's mill. His two daughters, Mary and Sarah Jane, worked as drawers for the firm of Sugden & Briggs, also in the mill complex. Mary earned 7s 6d a week whilst Sarah Jane was a half-timer, working part of the day in the mill and spending the rest of the day in school, earned 3s 6d, though their colleague, James Nicholls told the court that their wages would soon have risen to 11s and 9s respectively. This was an important consideration since

Town Hall, Leeds

most families at the time relied heavily on children's earnings to support the family. Henderson also had five other, younger, children to look after. The two girls worked from six in the morning to half past five or six at night. After their death the Ripley firm paid their funeral expenses and gave seven weeks wages as compensation.

The court heard that Sir Henry Ripley, who had died in 1882, had acted almost as his own architect, but in the end the judge decided:

> *'That the owners did all that unpractical men could be expected to do under the circumstances and therefore we do not attach any blame to them or find them guilty of negligence and we give as our verdict accidental death. We are of the opinion that the foundation was good, and that the fall of the chimney was partly due to the cutting, aided by the strong wind on the morning of the accident and we regret that the works were not stopped during the repairs.'*

Many of those who died were from the same family. Joseph and George Boldy, were two of five sons of Benjamin Boldy a blacksmith from Scotland. Urina and Walter Hicks were the eldest children of William Hicks of Cornwall, whilst Sarah and Lily Burley were the only two daughters of the family though there were five sons. Selina Woodhead, aged thirty-two, had only recently begun work in the mill, as had her daughter Susan. Both died there. Ellen Lumb died in the accident but her sister survived, as did their father, Shepherd Lumb.

Though there had been an unmarked commemorative stone, taken from the chimney itself, this eventually disappeared, so it was only in 2002 on the 120th anniversary of the event that a memorial stone naming those who died was finally erected near the site of the mill.

Those who died at the mill include:
Mary Hannah, eleven, Bowling Old Road daughter of Elijah Clifford, manager at Jonas Horsfall & Co.

Sarah Jane, eleven, referred to as Sarah Ann at the inquest but identified by her father, John Crowther.

Edgar North, twelve, Bowling Old Lane.

Lydia, twelve, daughter of David Lightowler, a van driver.

Hannah Eliza Narey, thirteen, Tennant Street.

Hartley Balmer, twelve, Bowling Old Lane. The family is listed as Bulmer in the 1881 census but Balmer at the inquest when his mother, Harriet, explained that she had identified the body from the clothing since the face was so badly crushed she 'dare not look upon it'. The coroner refused to accept this as sufficient and sent her back to view the body.

Emily, thirteen, Bowling Old Lane, daughter of Thomas Mitchell, a warp dresser.

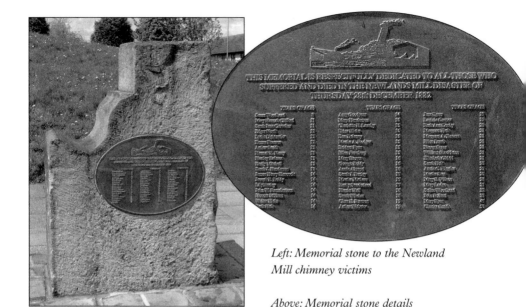

*Left: Memorial stone to the Newland
Mill chimney victims*

Above: Memorial stone details

Sarah J Henderson, thirteen, and her sister Mary, fifteen.

James Henry Hancock, fourteen.

Joseph E Boldy, fourteen, and his brother George, sixteen, Ripley Terrace,
  whose name was also given as 'Babby or Bilby' at the inquest.

John W Ramsbottom, fourteen, Cotewall Road.

Honoria M'Evans (McEvans), fourteen, Adelaide Street.

Walter, fourteen, and Urina Hicks, fifteen, Lower Round Street. Their
  father, William, was seriously injured and it was left to their mother,
  Jemima, to identify the bodies.

Ruth Firth, fourteen.

Amy Goodyear, fourteen, Moulson Street.

Charlotte Haslam Loasby, fifteen, named as Loasley on 1881 census, Town
  Hill Street, daughter of Thomas, a checker on the Great Northern
  Railway.

Dan Delaney, fifteen.

Martha A Rodger, fifteen.

Mary Brown, sixteen, Granby Street.

Annie Akroyd, sixteen, Calcutta Street, identified by her uncle John Akroyd.

Sarah Jane Burley, seventeen, and her sister Lily, fourteen, Tudor Street,
  Manchester Road.

Martha, seventeen, Grafton Street, daughter of Joseph Mathers.

Emily Sunderland, seventeen, Bengal Street.

Harriet Hall, eighteen, Cotewall Road.

Sarah Whelan, eighteen, nee Rock, of Duncan Street, Broomfields, who had been married only the previous month: 'When first discovered she was still alive and it may be a consolation to her parents and friends to know that the last rites of the Catholic Church to which she belonged, were administered before she expired.' Her husband, Patrick, an ironmoulder, gave evidence at the inquest.

Clara E Pearson, nineteen, and her sister, Emma, twelve, Ashley Street both identified by Mrs Emma Wright and Mrs Ann Wright, cousin and aunt of the deceased.

Arthur Webster, nineteen, son of Samuel Webster of Old Ashfield Place and brother-in-law of Mr W H Greenwood, one of the occupiers of the mills. His brother, Alfred Russell Webster appeared at the inquest. When Arthur was buried at Scholemoor cemetery his coffin was borne by members of the Alexandra Football Club, preceded by members of the 2nd West Riding Artillery Volunteers. He was a member of both groups.

Jane (or Jeannie) Egers (Agers), nineteen, Broadbent Street.

Lavinia, nineteen, Sloane Street, daughter of William Cooper.

Ruth Ann Denby, twenty, Baird Street.

Margaret Firth, twenty.

Margaret Ann Travers, twenty-one, single, of Caledonia Street.

Ellen, twenty-one, daughter of Shepherd Lumb, Tichborne Street, engineman, of Ripley's and Haley's.

Nancy Sagar (Sagars) twenty-one, Grafton Street. She was identified by her aunt, Elizabeth, wife of William Henry Hunt, the engine tenter.

William, twenty-one, Tudor Street son of Thomas Shackleton.

Elizabeth Oldrid, twenty-one, lived in Glover Street with her brother George but was identified by another brother, John, a foundryman from Mount Street.

Sarah, twenty-three, Clayton Lane wife of Alfred Holt.

Annie Catherine, twenty-three, wife of William Higgins of Granby Street.

Martha, twenty-five, wife of Henry Sant, a spinning overlooker, of Tennant Street.

Mary Ellen (Helen), twenty-eight, wife of George Wilson, Hardy Street.

Mary Lodge, thirty, unmarried, Caledonia Street.

Selina Woodhead, thirty-two, Elmsley Street and her daughter, Susan, eight, who was not employed at the mill but had just gone there to take her mother's breakfast in.

John Pollard, thirty-three, College Road, identified by his father-in-law, Jonas Taylor, a painter in Paisley Street, Horton.

Mary Allan Ryan, forty-five, and Bridget, fifteen, George Street. On 30 December *Bradford Daily Telegraph* gives these as 'Bridget Ryan an elderly woman and her daughter Mary Ryan' but the memorial reverses

these roles, so it appears that there was some confusion. Her brother Thomas Allen Ryan identified the bodies and commented that his sister had been 'deserted by her husband seventeen years ago'.
Charles Smith, fifty, and his son, Arthur, twelve, Little Cross Street.

The list of dead does not give all the story, however. The newspaper report often included the gory details of wounds received and tracked the progress of the injured. On 28 December the *Bradford Daily Telegraph*, named Grace Ellen Fawthrop of Parsonage Road as having 'injuries to head and system (hopeless case)'. On 3 January there was a report by Samuel Oddy of Park View, Manchester Road who worked as a fireman (one who was responsible for the boilers) for Messrs Haley & Co, who stated that he had realised that something was wrong and rushed out of the boiler house in order to 'get between the ashlar stones of the engine bed'. After the chimney fell he went back into the works, saw Grace Ellen and took her to the relative safety of the engine room where she was later found – and remained for sometime because the doctors were afraid that moving her would undoubtedly cause her death. Later she was taken to hospital and by 3 January she was 'partaking of refreshment and expected to recover' though she had a fractured skull and had lost an eye, but despite early hopes she died on 8 January. To add to the anguish of the family, her father, Ephraim Fawthrop, was seriously ill with pleurisy.

Another story related the tale of David Charles Brewer, son of David Jones Brewer, Round Street, Bowling Old Lane. He was pulled from the wreckage more than thirty hours after the chimney fell, when it was reported that, despite the danger, 'volunteers whose courage cannot be sufficiently praised' rushed to his rescue. Once they had made contact they gave him 'refreshments in the shape of brandy and other suitable articles'. Since the lad was only about ten years old, brandy may not have been the most suitable drink to give him. His two rescuers, G Ainsworth of Caledonia Street and Sam Fearnley of King Charles Street, managed to raise the beam, which had held him pinned down. He was largely unhurt from the episode and went off home to a good night's sleep. Early in January Pullan's Theatre of Varieties held a benefit performance for the relief fund which had been set up and David Brewer was taken on stage and presented with a gold watch by the owner, Mr Pullan.

Susannah Wright, sixteen, Calcutta Street, had a miraculous escape. Whilst having her breakfast, Susan Woodhead arrived with her mother's breakfast and should have brought some cotton for Susannah, but forgot. As a result Susannah ran back home to fetch it and was just about to return to the mill when the chimney fell.

Others injured included:
Robert Lord, wool buyer for Greenwoods; Miss Walsh, Caledonia Street; Mr

Baxter, engineer; Barry Ward, fourteen, Bramley Street; Smith Rhodes, sixty-three, Bolland Street; Kate Skelly, twenty-two, George Street; Annie Lawler, fifteen, Rydal Street; Harriot Crowther, fourteen, Cotewell Road; Alice Dixon, fourteen, Birch Street, Bowling Old Lane; Kate Wellman, fifteen, Darfield Street; Alice Freeman, twenty-one, Little Horton Lane; Lilian Osborne, nineteen, Laistridge Lane; Fred Dewhirst, thirty, Kings Wood Street; William Hall, twelve, Cotewell Road; Catherine Delaney, twenty-two, Granby Street, Broomfields; Henry Moore, twelve, Round Street, Bowling Old Lane; Mary Ann Wilson, fourteen, Tichborne Road; Ellie Towle, fifteen, Duncan Street; John Egarr, fifteen, Bottomley Street, Park Lane; John Edward Hall, fifteen, Cotewall Road (or Cotewell); Alice Hird, thirteen, Round Street; William Hicks, thirty-nine, Lower Round Street; Lizzie Walsh, sixteen, Caledonia Street; Ann Jane Bradley, eighteen, House Fold; Herbert Hudson, fifteen, Bowling Old Lane who was rescued by his brother William Henry; Robert Willey of Sloane Street.

Slightly injured:
Frederick Bendig, seventeen, St Stephen's Road; Hannah (or Anna) Jane Redman, eleven, a spinner from Bowling Old Lane who had managed to get under some machinery and then climbed out through a window. Lizzie Walsh, seventeen, spinner; Irving Wright, overlooker, Four Lane Ends; Tom Waddington Bowling Old Lane; ... Crowther, twelve, Cotewall Road; Mrs Farley, Grafton Street; ... Whiteley, Rydal Street; ... Taylor, Paisley Street; Willie Greenwood, Marygate.

[... indicates that no first name or gender was given in the newspaper report]

Sources:
Bradford Daily Telegraph 1882-4
Huddersfield Daily Examiner 1882-4
WYAS – Bradford records

5

Combs Colliery Disaster

Thornhill, Dewsbury

1893

Any major incident these days and we dip into our pockets for the disaster fund. Whether it is the desperate plight of the starving after failed rains in Africa or a man-made disaster when trains crash, we want to help. It is not a recent phenomenon. The local community has always helped out its less fortunate members and been prepared to support those further afield too. The subsequent relief funds provide considerable information for us.

Whilst mines these days have a good safety record, this wasn't always the case. A trip to the National Mining Museum for England, at Flockton, will quickly show you what it was like in the darkness, in cramped conditions using primitive tools and with limited safety precautions. Flooding, explosions and cave-ins were regular occurrences, often resulting in the loss of many lives.

On Tuesday 4 July 1893, 146 men went down to their work in Combs Mine, at Thornhill near Dewsbury. Only seven returned alive. There had been an explosion of 'fire-damp' or methane gas and, despite attempts to reach the men, the mine eventually had to be flooded to quench the fire.

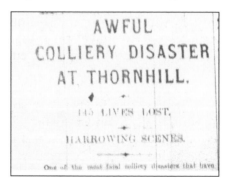

Headline, Huddersfield Daily Examiner

The first rescuers found eighty-six bodies:

> *'They were in groups, some of them looking as if calmly asleep, and others on their knees.'*

Eventually, a few men were brought out alive. These were:
Henry Wraithmell, of Thornhill Edge.
John Mallinson, of Middlestown.
John Garfitt, of Thornhill Edge.
Friend Senior, of Thornhill.
Squire Shires, of Middlestown.
Richard Wood, of Thornhill Edge.
Willie Lightowler, of Thornhill Edge.
Joshua Ashton, of Thornhill (who died two hours after rescue).
John Heywood, of Middlestown (who died on Thursday night).

The remaining bodies were recovered but it was a major tragedy for the area. Many of those who died came from the same family – fathers and sons, brothers and cousins. Close knit communities who had lost the main bread-winners. Immediately, the Local Boards such as from Thornhill, Ossett, and Dewsbury, together with ministers from churches and Methodist chapels, met to set up a Relief Fund for which the immediate aim was to provide temporary relief for widows etc. The amounts agreed were widows to receive 6s per week plus 2s 6d per week for each child under fifteen. Dependents other than widows also received some help. The final amounts paid from the Fund were 7s 6d per week for widows during their widowhood, with a sliding scale per child ranging from 3s 6d for one child under fifeen to 14s 6d for six children under fifteen. Dependent grandfathers and/or grandmothers or other dependents residing in the house would get one widow's allowance of 7s 6d whilst orphans also received 7s 6d up to age fifteen.

The list gives details of the families involved and includes the deceased's name, his age, the name and age of his wife; the total number of children, and how many were under fifteen. It also gives the village in which they lived. Other dependents such as aged parents or grandparents are also named.

Examples:
Booth, (alias Rusby) Charles, forty, wife Emma Rusby, thirty-eight, Smithy Brook, Middlestown, three children under fifteen. The 'remarks' column gives us the information that Charles was the father of Fred Booth and Henry Booth Nos 84 and 85 on the list.
Haigh Thomas, thirty-eight, wife Betsy Haigh, thirty-two, Whitley Lower. Three children under fifteen (two plus one expected). This was considered a

case of special need as Thomas was also supporting his father, Joseph, aged seventy and mother Jane, age sixty-eight.

Wood George, thirty-nine, Isabella, thirty-seven, Combs Thornhill. One child over fifteen, two children under fifteen. George was the father of J Wood, No 135, and was also supporting his father-in-law, James Rainey, sixty-four, and mother-in-law, Martha Rainey, sixty-three.

Details of single men and boys are also given. Many came from the same family as in the Booth family above. There are six men called 'Wood' though these were not necessarily all related, but Wraithmell is quite an unusual name so the two who died are probably related to the Henry who survived.

Some boys were the main stay of the household, such as Number 105 – Inman Hill, aged fourteen, who helped maintain the grandparents who had brought him up from infancy. His grandfather was unable to work so they were dependent on the wages of 15s brought home by their grandson.

Some of those who died have very little known about them. For example, number 110 was Joseph Johnson, aged sixteen, who lived with David Butcher of Whitley Lower. It was not known whether he had any parents living as he had come from the Ragged school at Bolton in Lancashire.

But this is not the only information that can be found from the records.

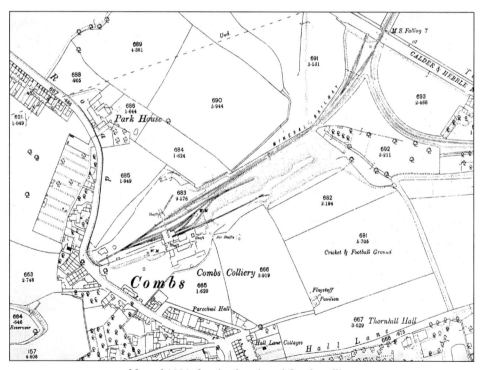

Map of 1893 showing location of Combs colliery

The amounts due were paid out over a period of time and this too is documented in the register – 'Record of the Widows, Children and Aged Parents Chargeable to the Fund'. Look up the man's number and you will find the payments given out to his dependents, listed per year together with the date on which payment ceased and the reason for stopping payment. Other information also comes to light.

Emma Rusby lost her widow's pension on 10 August 1895 when she married Jesse Speight. Her children continued receiving their payments until they each reached age fifteen – John William in 1897, Annie in 1901 and Florence Ann in 1904. Exact days are given so it must be assumed that this would be their fifteenth birthday – 8 July, 17 August and 25 July respectively.

When Betsy Haigh married Isaac Barker the register specifies that the widow's payment ceased on 14 August and that she married on that date. The date payment ceased is probably the marriage date for all the other widows who remarried, making finding the remarriage in the parish registers much easier. Betsy's date of birth is also given as 15 April 1861. As her first husband had been supporting his parents, Joseph and Jane Haigh, their payments ceased when they died. The register gives their dates of birth too.

When George Wood died, the details of his wife, family and in-laws were recorded but the payments register shows that his own mother, Sarah Wood, also received benefits until 29 January 1896 when she died. Her date of birth in 1831 is also given.

From these documents it is possible to track three generations, births, deaths and remarriages, which may explain that mystery of odd surnames appearing in a family.

Relief funds rarely just list the recipients of the money. The Subscribers' List gives details of the people who paid into the Fund and the amount paid. E T Ingham JP, of Blake Hall, Mirfield gave £1,000 and paid for the burial of the dead whilst the colliery owners of West Yorkshire gave £1,130. There were benefit events, just as there are today, including a cricket match between West Riding Police and Dewsbury Police which raised a sum of £100 and an Open Air Concert at Kippax which raised over £33. Many other mines and mining associations in the area donated to the fund and villages all around held their own fund raising events, donating the whole as a 'Local Fund' amount. Many of these local events list individual subscribers as well as totals from churches, chapels and work places. Towns and villages had collected money to pay for the celebrations for the marriage, on 6 July, of George V to Mary of Teck. The residue was often donated to the Relief Fund.

On 7 and 8 July the burial of many of the dead took place in Thornhill parish church. Surprisingly, there is no monument to this tragedy at the church, though it is currently being mooted.

Thornhill Church

Sources:

West Yorkshire Archives, Kirklees, reference number WYK 1055/4/3

Huddersfield Daily Examiner 1893

Those who died were:

John Ashton
Charles Booth (alias Rusby)
Aquila Brook
Charles Brook
Charles Brook
Henry Burton (alias Halstead)
Edwin Butcher
Mark Butcher
Joseph Coates
John Croft
George Crossley
Samuel Crossley
Stephen Drake
Tom Dyson
John Ellis
Tom Ellis
William Ellis
Edward Fearnley
George Fenton
Ezra Field
Charles Firth
Eli Firth
Charles Fisher
George Fisher
William Goldthorpe, sen
William Goldthorpe, jun
Thomas Haigh
Henry Halstead
William Hampshire
John Hardcastle
Amos Hawksworth
John Heywood
James Hill
Edward Hinchliffe
Jonathan Hinchliffe
William Jackson
Matthew Jessop
Lewis Lee
Isaac Lightowler

John Henry Longbottom
George Milnes
James Noble
Richard Pickard
Abraham Ramsden
Benjamin Ramsden
David Ramsden
Matthew Ramsden
Charles Rusby (alias Booth)
James Scargill
Lot Scargill
Robert Scargill
Lot Senior
John William Smith
Mark Smith
Herbert Speight
James Joseph Steadman
Henry Summerscales
William Henry Swallow
John Tindall
George Wilcock
Walton Henry Oxley Wilcock
George Wilkinson
George Wood
Sam Wood
William Wood
William Varley Wroe
Josiah Roberts
Joshua Ashton
Herbert Asquith
Samuel Croft
Rowland Blakeley Garfitt
Walter Hardcastle
Henry Lightowler
Joseph Little
Benjamin Milnes
Edward Mort
Benjamin Secker
Alexander Andrews
Oliver Ashton
Ephraim Beaumont

John William Beaumont	Frederick Kendall
Lister Beaumont	Sykes Lee
George Gilbert Brown	John William Little
William Brown	Smith Longbottom
Fred Booth (alias Rusby)	Leonard Milner
Henry Booth (alias Rusby)	Richard Milner
Willie Brook	Fransford Milnes
Alfred Butcher	James Milnes
George Henry Butcher	John Buckley Netherwood
Seth Butcher	Joseph Noble
Willie Coates	Arthur Oates
William Coles	Fred Oates
George Chapman	Stanley Pickles
William Dawson	William Ramsden
Frank Douglas	Alfred Alonzo Ramsden
Herbert Dunford	Fred Rusby (alias Booth)
Edward Fearnley, jun	Henry Rusby (alias Booth)
Walter Field	Joseph Scarfe
Alfred Firth	Rufus Scargill
George Firth	Ernest Sheard
Samuel Firth	John William Smith
John Fox	William Stephenson
Thomas Fox	Lambert Thornes
Arthur Grimsdell	Thomas Watkins
Frank Haigh	Friend Wood
Inman Hill	John Wood
Thomas Stanley Hill	Joseph Wood
Harry Hinchcliffe	William Wood
George Walter Holland	Herbert Wraithmell
Harry Jessop	Willie Wraithmell
Joseph Johnson	John James Wright

6

Factory Fire at H Booth & Sons

Huddersfield

1941

On the morning of 31 October 1941, many people in Huddersfield were making their way to work. Factories were still operating, often converted to make different products for the war – army blankets, army uniform cloth or munitions.

At 7.30am Joe Wood, who was in charge of the boilers, arrived at H Booth & Co, a large clothing factory in the centre of Huddersfield, near the Empire Cinema. He heard two of the firewatchers at the stove on the floor above the offices, but didn't speak to them. Instead he checked his boilers, cleared out the clinker and by 7.45 he had turned on the steam and switched on the

Empire Cinema, Huddersfield. Booth's factory was next to this building

electric current, ready for work to begin at eight o'clock.

At the same time, Wilfred Booth, the managing director, arrived, going up to his office to open the post. He heard people moving around but assumed they were the firewatchers and Joe Wood tending the boilers.

Within a short while the workers, mainly women, began to arrive, greeting each other, clocking in and going up to their usual work area. Vera Fisher, Rosaline Lovidge, Hilda Bevins, Annie Mitchell, Florrie Fox, Doris Pennington and Minnie Netherwood headed up to the second floor, as Doris's sister, Helena, and their friends, Mabel Mellor and Annie Harrop, carried on up to the third. Others soon joined them until the bell to start work was heard over their chatter. A few minutes later one of them called out that there was a fire somewhere. It hardly seemed possible at that time in the morning but the women set off down the main staircase to see what was happening. Doris tried at first to go up to the third floor but suddenly realised the smoke was getting thicker and turned back, stopping only to help another employee, Mrs Scaley, who had fallen.

Vera Fisher too tried to reach the third floor but was pulled back and headed instead down the main staircase, passing Mr Thirkill who was trying to put out the flames with a fire extinguisher. He shouted at them to get out

Old Infirmary buildings, now part of Huddersfield Technical College

of the building and returned to his fire fighting.

Outside on the pavement, passers-by were rushing to help. Many of the girls who were trapped on the upper floors jumped to try to escape the flames, only to perish on the concrete below.

Tom Thornton, an engineer of Wheathouse Road, Birkby saw an injured woman lying unconscious on the pavement. He picked her up and put her into a motorcar, which took her to the Royal Infirmary. There she regained consciousness and gave her name as Edie Lockwood. She was one of the first casualties to be taken to the infirmary along with Barbara Chadwick. They both survived but many others died soon after arriving at the hospital. The vast majority of the injuries were fractures, probably caused by jumping from windows. Few at this stage suffered burns.

The majority of the employees succeeded in escaping from the building before the fire had spread to any great extent and they were taken to the canteen of Messrs Bairstow, Son & Co Ltd wholesale clothing manufacturers in FitzWilliam Street, who provided them with refreshments. It was feared that eighteen people had been killed, but this figure kept rising throughout the day as more and more employees failed to answer the roll call. By eleven o'clock twenty-six had been unaccounted for, and by the next morning forty-seven were believed to have died.

The Lord Lieutenant of Yorkshire, the Earl of Harewood, received a telegram from the King, which was forwarded to the Mayor:

```
The King's Telegram

The Queen and I are shocked to hear of the disaster at the clothing
factory in Huddersfield in which so many girls lost their lives.
Please convey our deepest sympathy to the bereaved relatives.
His Majesty the King
```

An inquest was quickly arranged, though:

> *'Only a few of the bodies could be identified in the ordinary way. The rest of the victims, whose remains are said to have been burnt beyond recognition, had to be identified by portions of clothing or by articles found on or near them.'*

PCs Alfred James Adams, Frederick Harwood, William Alfred Smallwood, Herbert Oldroyd, Wilfred John Ayling, John Cheslett, Robert Hudspith, Jack Hague, James McCann, Frederick Terry, Edward Moxon and Edward Midwood all gave their evidence of finding the various victims. PC Frank

Holdsworth confirmed that he took Doris Gatenby and Gladys Gwendoline Marshall to the infirmary where they later died; PC F R Wilds took Ann Woodhouse and Fred Platt there too. Fred Platt survived but Ann later died. PC Simeon Mounsey had the unhappy task of identifying the body of his fifteen-year-old daughter, Betty.

Harold Smith, of Albert Terrace, Linthwaite, who lost his two daughters, Freda and Jean, said he had not seen Freda since she left home to go to work but he was able to identify the body of Jean by certain articles including her metal identity tag. The coroner then commented that it was a good idea to wear such tags, especially in the 'present conditions'. He was of course referring to the fact that Britain was at war and suffering regular air raids, rather than fires from other causes.

In many cases the relatives came forward to state that they had not seen the missing person since they left for work on the morning of the disaster – nothing could be found to positively identify the remains, though nowadays a DNA test would resolve the matter. It was probably for this reason that it was eventually decided to bury the majority in a mass grave in the town cemetery at Edgerton.

Over a series of meetings the whole story gradually became known.

Among those present at the inquest were Mr A W Garrett, Chief Inspector of Factories, Minister of Labour and National Service; Mr E L Macklin, Superintending Inspector of Factory of the Ministry of Labour; Miss A D E Bunch, Local Factory Inspector; the Chief Constable, Mr James Chadwick, Miss Annie Houghlin, National Organisation of the Tailors and Garment Workers Union and Mr Perry Burns, local organiser of that union. Mr C W Nelson, of Leeds, represented Messrs Booth and Sons Ltd.

Miss Whitely, of Swallow Lane, Golcar, cashier for Booth & Co, produced the wages book but could not say which of the employees were on the premises at the time of the fire. PC Harry Adams, Coroner's Officer, produced a list of employees of Booth's, which he had compared with the wages book. He said:

> 'The total number of employees was twenty-eight males and ninety-six females. Of these there were absent from work on October 31, five males and twenty-nine females. Twelve males and thirty-six females escaped. Eight males and thirteen females who lost their lives had been identified. Three males and twenty-three females were not identified.'

The coroner then wanted to 'set the scene' for the jury so called in Norman Gulley, a well-known Huddersfield architect. He did not think the building had ever had an external staircase but confirmed that the partitions in the building were of wood and glass. When asked if they were inflammable, he replied 'definitely'. The factory building was a five storey one, a main staircase ran through the building and two other staircases, one of which ran from the ground floor to the first floor only; the other from the ground floor to the top of the building. The building was constructed of internal steel frame and floors of timber. Staircases of wood and a hoist encased in wood except in the basement and at the top where it was encased in brick, but if the hoist had got on fire at the bottom it would burn fiercely and quickly. He also stated that steel pillars ran through the building and it would have been better if they were encased in concrete, since they could have played a part in the collapse of the building through the effect of heat on them. He had prepared the plans for the air raid shelter and the air raid shelter was still intact after the fire.

Next came George Andrew Nicol, engineer's surveyor, of Leeds who had made external examination of the steam boilers and steam irons in September and found them in perfect order. He had also examined the steam boiler and water-heating boiler since the fire and they were in perfect order. It was quite clear that no explosion took place.

Ernest Jenkinson, a joiner, from Newsome, told how he put in a wooden staircase from the second to the third floor in January 1939. The lining on the walls of the ground floor was red wood and varnished – a highly inflammable combination.

The boiler man, Joe Wood, went on to explain that after starting up the boilers as usual, he met George Thirkill at the foot of the stairs in the basement. His clothes were on fire:

'and I threw an overcoat over him and took him outside the building into Fountain Street, through the goods entrance.'

He saw four girls lying on the ground. By this time the 'factory was blazing fiercely'. He stated that the boiler usually worked at 60lb pressure but that morning it was only at 30lb pressure because they had received instructions from the AFS [Auxiliary Fire Service] men in a fire drill to reduce the pressure.

Given the uncertainty of the times it is not surprising that the jury were suspicious; 'did you see anyone follow George Thirkill into the basement?' they asked, to which Joe emphatically replied: 'No.'

Peter Beardsell, a clothier's fitter and Alfred Beaumont confirmed that they had been there at the start of the fire, thinking at first it was confined to the fitting room. They had both gone to investigate, finding Mr Booth using the firm's fire extinguishers on the fire. As Mr Senior appeared, Booth shouted: 'Call the fire brigade.' Senior went to do so, whilst Beardsell ran for more fire fighting equipment from the top floor. He found everyone there working normally and shouted to George Woffenden that the shop was on fire and everyone had to get out. By the time he got back down the stairs, the smoke was beginning to choke him so he ran down the main staircase and out at the front of the building. In his opinion, if the girls on the top floor had followed him down, they would have survived, though he admitted that the smoke had already been very thick. It was also suggested that as he had a reputation for practical jokes, they might have thought he was joking but this was strenuously denied. It was more likely that the girls could not see that the stairs were clear and had been afraid to follow him down. He confirmed that Booth had said to call the fire brigade, but nothing about sounding any alarm. Beardsell could not remember the last time they'd had a fire drill.

It was then the turn of Wilfred Booth, the Managing Director of the firm. His firm had been in the building over ten years and there had never been any outside fire escape. The Sanitary Inspector, under the provisions of the Factory Act, had examined the building. A certificate was issued but this was now destroyed. On being asked, Ernest Richardson, Chief Sanitary Inspector admitted that an assistant inspected the premises on 26 April 1939, when it was decided the fire escapes were OK. On 3 May 1939, a certificate was authorised but not issued owing to lack of staff. The premises could have been cleared in three minutes if a timely alarm was given. An outside staircase was not necessary provided the work people were given adequate instructions. Dennis Drake, assistant sanitary inspector, confirmed he had thought the fire escapes reasonable.

Booth continued, saying that soon after his arrival, he heard a crackling and went to the fitting room where he saw a fire in the corner to the right of the door, where there was a coat stand with an overcoat and a gabardine coat. Flames were already rising to the ceiling from these coats. Booth immediately started to use a fire extinguisher on the flames. He was shortly to be joined by Mr Carter, the warehouse foreman who brought a second fire extinguisher. Later, Mr Senior arrived but by then the fire was spreading, so Booth shouted to ring the fire brigade. The smoke became so thick they couldn't see.

The fire signal was on the telephone system and operated a buzzer on every floor. It had been used before the war, for signalling but he gave instructions for it not to be used since the war, though it had been used occasionally. It had been used the day before the fire. It sounded very different to the telephone but it was possible that it was out of action because of the fire. The danger signals were seven blasts on the buzzer.

The question of Mr Booth's conversation with the police in the immediate aftermath of the fire arose. Booth said he did not remember telling Sergeant Watson that the fire was caused by Mr Senior's tobacco pipe setting fire to his coat. He eventually admitted that he did make that statement but took it out because: 'I felt I had no right to assume that.'

When asked if there had been a previous fire, he initially answered: 'No,' but qualified this by saying that there had been a smoking coat but not an actual fire, about twelve months previously. The smouldering coat had been Mr Senior's and a pipe in the pocket had caused the damage. Smoking was not allowed on the premises – though nothing seemed to have been done about the initial incident. The coat rack had not been moved since no one thought anything else would happen. Booth agreed that he didn't tell anyone to give a warning when the fire actually broke out – he'd been too occupied with fire fighting.

William Rhodes Senior said that he arrived at five minutes to eight, putting his grey tweed coat on the coat stand along with a lady's long coat and a gabardine. He was closely questioned over his actions:

> *'Was your pipe in your pocket?'*
> *'Yes.'*
> *'When was it put there?'*
> *'On entering the building.'*
> *'Were you smoking before then?'*
> *'Yes.'*

Senior stated that he knocked the ashes out of the pipe and blew through it. He was sure it was clear. After he started work, Mr Waite shouted that the office was on fire. He called the fire brigade and pressed the alarm, which should have sounded the buzzers, but he was not sure if it did. Notices were on every floor regarding fire alarm procedures.

He agreed that his pipe had caused the incident a year ago, but he had been very particular since then.

Finally, the coroner summed up the evidence before the jury retired to consider their verdict. He said that there was no need to make remarks on the origin of the fire or on a previous similar incident. The fire spread rapidly, probably because of the wood construction. An alarm was given. Mr Booth acted naturally in trying to extinguish the fire before calling the brigade as he thought it was just a small fire. He criticised the Corporation, saying that the certificate should have been issued. It was not fair to firms or to the Inspector of Factories to withhold the certificate.

After a short discussion a verdict of accidental death was brought in.

Mr Booth expressed his sympathy with relatives and workers as he had 'been associated with many of them nearly all his life and his sorrow was greater than words could express'.

On 6 December the local newspaper commented that this was a 'Tragedy of Errors' with lots of 'if only's' but it was no use looking with hindsight. But there was a slackness in the organisation of the firm – there had been no fire drills recently – two workers had not heard any signals during the time they worked there. There was considerable conflict of opinion as to whether an outside fire escape was needed or not, but if the fittings were so inflammable, then surely there was a greater need for a proper escape and this should have been noted.

The Policeman's Part

It was also pointed out in the newspapers that tragedies of this sort have to be dealt with by the police:

> *'The police have had the task of 'mothering' (if one may put it that way) relatives who have been so tragically bereaved, receiving them at the police station, visiting them for the purpose of interview and identification and generally fulfilling the role of both official and friend in need.*
> *From all I hear, the men of the Huddersfield Borough Police who have had to perform this sad duty have done so with a sympathy and tact which merit the highest praise. Most touching of all has been the gratitude expressed by the relatives themselves who in their sorrow have spoken a 'thank you' to the man in blue.'*

Later, Police Commendations went to Inspector John R Braithwaite, Sergeant Lewis W Crossley, Constables Harry Adams, Vincent Molloy and John W Cottingham.

The Funerals

A memorial service was held in the parish church, broadcast over loudspeakers, as was the later committal. The streets were lined with thousands of people, all standing silently, men with hats doffed as the deceased, each in a separate hearse and coffin, were driven slowly past. Buses were provided to take all the mourners out to Edgerton and then back to the Town Hall. At the cemetery there were hundreds of wreaths – a huge shield of white chrysanthemums with a red cross of carnations from the Textile & Clothing Contractors Association; a white cross of roses and carnations from the Mayor and Council; a harp of red carnations and white chrysanthemums from the staff of H Booth & Co. Over 700 mourners surrounded the communal grave. The service was conducted by the Mayor's Chaplain, Rev E Clarke, the minister from the Buxton Road Methodist Chapel, Rev William Hardwick and Fr D McGillycuddy and Fr Ryan from St Joseph's RC Church. Fr McGillycuddy blessed the grave and Flanders poppies were dropped onto the coffins.

Police and other officials praised the members of the public who all quietly filed passed the grave, yet, despite there being thousands of people there, no damage was done to flowers or other grave plots in the area. Though the cost of the funeral was borne by the council, a subscription had been started for a

Huddersfield Parish Church

suitable memorial for the victims and this provoked much speculation. The council finally decided that whilst the bulk of the money should be distributed to the relatives of the victims, a substantial memorial would be placed over the grave, with any remaining money being put towards something suitable such as named beds in the infirmary.

The fire victims, commemorated on the memorial in Edgerton Cemetery:

Miss Doris Gatenby, Alder Street, Fartown
Miss Gladys Gwendoline Marshall, Paddock Foot
Miss Betty Mounsey, Springdale Street
Mrs Eileen Leadbeater, Bradley Boulevard Sheepridge
Miss Ann Woodhouse, Town End, Almondbury
Miss Edie Lockwood, Cliff Hill, Shelley
Leonard Moorhouse, Cadogan Avene, Lindley
John Christopher Hanselman, Clough Road, Birkby
Nellie Pugh, Eldon Road, Marsh
Jean Smith, Charles Ave, Manchester Road, and her sister, Freda Smith

Edgerton Cemetery and chapel

Mabel Mellor, Crosland Hill Road

Joan Doughty, Walpole Road, Crosland Moor. She was only fourteen and had
    begun work at the factory only the day before the fire. It was her first job.

Edith Whitton, Chapel Lane, Milnsbridge

Kate Richardson, Clauyton Fields, Birkby

Lilian Watmuff, Farfield Road, Almondbury

Agnes Hoyle, Ashenhurst Road, Newsome

Marion Kaye, Watercroft, Almondbury

Jean Wilson, KayeLane, Almondbury

Mabel Simpson, Northgate, Almondbury

Horace Binnie, Farfield Road, Almondbury

Annie Bentley, Brick and Tile Terrace, Rastrick

Lizzie Staveley, Meal Hill, Slaithwaite

Joan Netherwood, Woodside Farm, Grange Moor

Mildred Beaumont, Grove Yard, Lepton

Memorial to the fire victims, Edgerton Cemetery

Gladys Parker, Bedford Avene, Grange Moor
Arthur Senior, Liversedge
Helena Pennington, Battye Avene, Crosland Moor
Cissie Harrop, Heaton Road, Paddock
Joyce Hornsey, Holme Place, Marsh
Florence Wood, Quarmby Road
Marie Holt, Rosedale Avenue, Modlgreen
Margaret Shaw, Hall Cross Road, Lowerhouses
Margaret Birkhead, Dewhurst Road, Fartown
Mary Scarramuzza, Alder Street, Fartown
Gladys Butterworth, Clayton Fields, Birkby
Joan Butler, Bradford Road
Annie Taylor, Bradford Road
Walter Beaumont, Belle Vue Crescent, Sheepridge
Charlie Atkinson, Leymoor Road, Golcar

Henry Dransfield, St Helen's Road, Almondbury
George Sanderson, Meltham Mills Road, Meltham
Olive Blakelock, Newsome Road
Jessie Beaumont, Alice Row, Paddock
Jim Woffenden, Bramston Sttreet, Radstrick
Percy Boothroyd, Handel Street, Golcar
George Matthewman Hutchinson, Eleanor Street, Fartown

Source:
Huddersfield Daily Examiner 1941

Part 2

Leisure Time

7

Masbro' Boat Disaster

Rotherham

1841

Walk around Rotherham Minster Church (previously Parish Church of All Saints) and it will not be long before you see a beautifully carved marble memorial with a long list of fifty names. Look closer and you will see that only three of those remembered there were adults. This was not the result of some industrial disaster involving child labour, but a day of celebration that quickly turned to tragedy.

Boat builders Chambers and Son of Masbro' (Masbrough) had been commissioned to build a new boat at their boatyard on Forge Lane, for Henry Cadman of Sheffield and Robert Marsh of Doncaster. By 14 July 1841 the John & William was ready to be launched into the River Don where the river

is so narrow that boats had to be launched sideways: a traditional method which had never caused any problems before. However, the John & William was slightly different. It was of a type known as a 'billy boy' – a flat-bottomed coastal vessel, mainly used on the east coast. But they were usually only 5 feet 6 inches in height from the keel to the deck but this one was 7 feet high. This shouldn't have made such a lot of difference but it may have made the boat less stable.

Another tradition in the area was to fill the boat with people, especially children, who particularly enjoyed the excitement of the day, the flags flying, the gathering

Memorial plaque in Rotherham Minster

speed of the boat sliding down the slipway and the massive splash as it hit the water. Families and neighbours gathered on the banks to watch the spectacle as the boat filled with boys, many playing truant from the nearby school. There were superstitions too. No members of the owner's family were allowed on board and no women; they would bring bad luck to the launch.

A glorious morning set the scene for the long awaited launch. As soon as the boat was full of cheering, eager children the signal was given and the supports at each end of the boat were struck away. One end freed immediately and the boat began to move, but the other end stuck. On deck, the boys ran to see what was happening and the sudden increase in weight on one side of the boat caused it to keel over and submerge into the river. 'Their joy was transformed into despair and a thrill of horror prevailed all around' an eyewitness wrote to the Rotherham Advertiser in later years.

Some were fortunate. They were thrown from the boat as it turned over and landed close to the opposite bank, where willing hands dragged them ashore. As always, the courageous appeared. George Langthorne leapt into the icy water to rescue some of the boys and John Johnson of Doncaster Gate was seen to dive down three times and each time bring two of the boys to safety. William Freeman also dived, desperately searching for his sons: Samuel, aged sixteen, and little William junior, who was only eight. Their father saved at least five boys, but both his own lads perished. Another family who suffered more than one loss was that of John Smith, a waterman who had taken his two sons, Charles and Henry, to the event. All were lost, leaving his widow, Ann with their small daughter, Miranda, who was only one year old. Henry Newsome, a carpenter, was luckier. He jumped in and managed to save his son, Henry junior, who was only nine. His daughter, Ann, who worked as a nurse for the Hague family had an equally lucky escape. She had taken John Hague to see the launch but had been 'seized with a presentiment of danger' and left the ship before the launch.

Then matters became even worse. The owner, Mr Chambers, desperately hoping to help, shouted that the people must be saved and to sacrifice the boat if need be. Captain George Taylor of the John & Joseph and a builder who was nearby climbed onto the keel and tried to axe a hole through to the trapped victims but air getting into the boat simply made it sink deeper. Many blamed this single action for the greater loss of life.

Everyone rallied round. With a typical Victorian approach, brandy to refresh the survivors was sent by Joshua Crosland of the Waggon & Horses, William Flockton of the Hammer & Vice and Mrs Horsfield of the Ship Inn. The Quarter Session court, which was being held nearby, had to be halted as people flocked to the area and the police were needed to hold back the crowds, some just trying to get a glimpse of the action, others crying desperately for their children.

About half of the boys who died went to the British School, which was nearby. One lad was heard to say that: 'Mr Sharp, our worthy schoolteacher, did not give us a holiday or make any reference [to the launch] so half the school played truant and went to the launch.' Rotherham also had a charity school known as the Feoffee's School, providing education for poor boys. The master of the school, John Mycock, who lived nearby at the Crofts, was quick to write to the newspaper refuting the suggestion that some of his boys had been killed, since 'not one Charity boy was present upon the sad occasion'. No doubt the trustees would have asked questions if those receiving charity had absented themselves for such a frivolous reason. There were some positive events though. John Bletcher, aged fourteen years, was pulled out unconscious but awoke later in his home in Roger Lane, Hollowgate.

Many of the dead were buried at the parish church where the bells were muffled and tolled for three days. Others were buried at the Independent chapel in Masbrough on College Road. This is now a warehouse and few of the gravestones can be seen. Most are in appalling condition. Only one

Gravestone of the Earnshaw family

gravestone referring to this event is still legible – that of George Earnshaw, whose mother, Ann, died the year after her son:

> *'Sacred to the memory of George son of William and Ann Earnshaw who awfully perished with forty-nine others at the launching of a vessel in Masbro' on the 5th July 1841 aged 7 years and [8?] months. Also the above named Ann Earnshaw who departed this life June 4th 1842 aged 40 years.'*

Subscriptions were called for to help the families and in the days following the disaster the newspapers listed all those who gave a donation. The managing committee included: Thomas Badger, who was also the coroner overseeing the inquests, Andrew Crawshaw, (treasurer) watchmaker and jeweller; William Beatson, chemist; John Aldred, chemist; Rev James Bromley; William Earnshaw; Benjamin Badger, auctioneer; G W Chambers; Thomas Law, linen and woollen draper; William Bingley; George Taylor; Frederick Fleck, iron merchant; George Hutchinson; Francis Parker; William Wingfield; C S R Sandford, fire iron manufacturer (of Sandford & Yates); Alexander Grant; George Knowles; John Graves Clark; Richard Haggard; John Barras. All these men also served on the inquest jury except George Knowles, Richard Haggard and John Barras.

Across Masbrough cemetery where many victims were buried

The inquest, held at the *Angel* pub in High Street, eventually brought in a verdict of 'accidental death' on those who died, but the boat owners also had to pay a 'deodand' of one shilling. A deodand is a forfeit to the Crown, usually given to charity, when an animal or object, in this case the boat, has caused a death. Not surprisingly at a later meeting of the local council it was recommended that in future shipyards should ensure 'the entire exclusion of all unnecessary persons, but especially children, from their vessels at the time of a launch'.

Details of those who perished:

Thomas, ten, Masbro' Common, son of Ann Straw, widow.

Charles, eleven, Masbro' Common, son of John Robinson, shaft maker.

James, fifteen, Masbro', son of John Argot, carter.

John, fifteen, Masbro', son of Benjamin Brown, labourer.

Joseph, twelve, Pool Green, son of Robert Furniss, miller.

Thomas, thirteen and William, eleven, Pool Green, sons of Joseph Woodger, chainmaker.

George, seven, Pool Green, son of William Earnshaw, moulder.

John Jacques, eleven, Jubb's Fold, son of Ann Green, wife of John Green, blacksmith.

Charles, twelve, Masbro', son of Joseph Hamby, blacksmith.

John Fox, sixteen, Masbro', a moulder, parents dead.

William, ten and Alfred, five, Back Lane, Masbro', sons of Septimus and Elizabeth Greenfield, boat hauler.

William, ten, New Holland, son of Joseph Bowler, flax dresser.

Thomas, seven, New Holland, son of Joseph Dale, potter.

Thomas, fifteen, Old Holland, moulder, son of Eliza (Elizabeth) Bradbury, widow.

John, thirteen, son of George Haywood.

John, seventeen, Rawmarsh Lane, son of Samuel Gillott, labourer.

John Smith, forty, waterman of Rawmarsh Lane and his two sons, Charles, eight and Henry, five.

George, sixteen, Rawmarsh Lane, waterman, son of Isaac Curtis, porter.

Samuel, sixteen and William, eight, Rawmarsh Lane, sons of William Freeman, waterman.

George, fourteen, Tinsley lock, son of W Ramsden, shoemaker.

Richard, seventeen, Masbro', labourer.

John Greatorix, twenty-one, Furnival Street, Sheffield, joiner, son of Harriet Taylor, wife of Benjamin Taylor, mason.

Charles, fourteen, Wellgate, son of George Mathews, hauler.

Samuel, eighteen, Wellgate, labourer, son of Benjamin Woodhouse, moulder.

John, fourteen and Richard, nine, Wellgate, sons of Jonathan and Elizabeth Shillitto, stay maker.

Joseph, ten, Quarry Hill, son of John Earnshaw, mason.

John, ten, Wellgate, son of John Pattison, sawyer.

William Hall, nine, Wellgate, son of George Hall, labourer.

George, seven, Wellgate, son of George Nixon, labourer.

Andrew, nine, Wellgate, son of George Dobson, fishmonger.

Henry, eight, Wellgate, son of George and Sarah Goodall.

William, fourteen, Wellgate, son of Robert and Jane Bradshaw, flax dresser.

David, thirteen, Pigeon Lane, son of Robert Cundell, shoemaker.

Henry, eight, Pigeon Lane, son of William Crowther.

John, ten, Market Place, son of John Kent, wheelwright.

Joseph Buckley, thirty-three, Oil Mill Fold, joiner and his son Alfred, six.

Samuel Heathcote, forty-one, Crofts, joiner and bell ringer at the parish church.

Robert, thirteen, Westgate, son of Joseph and Sarah Lancaster, currier.

Samuel, ten, Westgate Green, son of Samuel and Elizabeth Dobbs, publican and mason.

Stephen W Blackburn, fourteen, Westgate, son of Thomas Blackburn.

John, nineteen, Westgate, waterman, son of Thomas Parrott.

James, eleven, Crofts, son of James Yates.

William, eleven, Masbro', son of Joseph Wood, waterman.

Inscriptions (other than the list of names) from the memorial in Rotherham Minster Church:

In Memory of the fifty young persons
Whose names are inscribed on this tablet
Who awfully perished at the launching of a vessel
At Masbrough July 3rd 1841

By the generous sympathy of their fellow townsmen and others
A fund was raised to relieve the families bereaved by this sad calamity
And to erect this monumental record
In humble and reverent recognition of the divine will,
As an admonitory warning to the living
And a memorial of condolence to those
Whose hearts and hopes
Were thereby suddenly bow'd to the dust

★★★

They sank not in the storm toss'd wave
Crested by oceans surge
Where billows murmuring o'er their grave
Would sound a ceaseless dirge

Imprisoned by the inverted bark
Beneath the waveless stream
They drank death's bitter cup, life's spark
Was quench'd, dispell'd its dream

Their tombs are clos'd, the muffled peal
Has rung their funeral knell
What eye can see beyond the veil
Where now their spirits dwell

Mourners in faith flee to the cross
Thence living waters flow
A healing balm for every loss
Sure refuge from your woe'

'Think ye those eighteen, upon whom the tower of Siloam fell and slew them, that they were sinners above all men that dwelt in Jerusalem? I tell you, Nay: but except ye repent ye shall all likewise perish.' Luke 13:4

Edwin Smith, the sculptor of the monument worked as a stonemason at Sheffield General Cemetery. His son, Theophilus, was also a sculptor and photographer in the city.

Sources:
Minster Church of Rotherham memorial plaque
Sheffield and Rotherham Independent Newspaper 1841
Rotherham Advertiser 1883
Rotherham Metropolitan Borough, Archives and Local Studies Section
1841 Census

8

Drowning at Newby Park

Near Knaresborough

1869

Some disasters involve great loss of life, some have disastrous conse-quences for the families involved. Such a disaster happened in 1869 when the York And Ainsty Hunt met one fine Thursday morning in February. The lead was taken by Sir Charles Slingsby, master of the hounds, riding his oldest and favourite hunter, *Saltfish*, with William Orvis, the first whip, close behind. Eventually they found a fox and chased it hard for over an hour, until they neared Newby Hall where Lady Mary Vyner lived. The fox quickly crossed the River Ure, followed by the hounds, but the horsemen were rather daunted by the fast flowing water. The markers for river depth had already disappeared under the surging river so, whilst some rode further upstream to find the ford, many called for the ferry to come over for them.

Swollen by the late rains, and to a great extent diverted from its natural channel, the river swept along with a strong deep current at this point, about 50 or 60 yards wide. As soon as the boat, steered by the Newby Hall gardener and his son, reached them, the master of the hounds urged his horse into the boat and this example was followed by around fifteen or sixteen men with their horses, who crowded into a vessel intended for only half this number. Those who entered the boat were: Sir Charles Slingsby, Orvis (the whip) Sir George Wombwell, Captain Vyner, Mr Clare Vyner, Mr Lloyd, Mr Robinson, Major Mussinden, Captain Molyneux, the Hon Henry Molyneux, Captain Key, Mr White and a number of other York officers. Viscount Downe, Lord Lascelles and several others, who were either unable to find room in the boat or had doubts as to its safety, remained on the bank awaiting its return.

Seizing the chain by which the flat-bottomed boat was propelled, Captain Vyner and his brother pushed off from the riverside and sent the vessel right into the stream. Reports become confused about what happened next. One witness stated that the chain, which was used to propel the boat across the river and back, was fixed in the 'down stream' position when it should have

Newby Hall, near Ripon

been turned to 'up stream'. Some suggest that Sir Charles Slingsby's horse became restive and kicked the animal belonging to Sir George Wombwell, which returned the kick and the animals began to panic. Others state that old Saltfish simply jumped out of the boat into the river dragging Sir Charles with him.

Whatever the initial cause, the boat swayed first to one side and then to the other and finally it was turned bottom upwards, trapping the men and horses underneath. For a moment the slimy bottom of the boat was all that could be seen by the horror-stricken spectators on the bank, then here and there in different parts of the stream heads began to appear only to sink again, their owners shouting out for help and desperately grasping at anything that seemed to float. The horses battled with the current, striking out with all their energy, while they and their riders were swept out of reach by the current.

Those watching who could swim plunged in to try to save their friends whilst others tied whips together, throwing them towards the drowning men or throwing heaps of wood from the banking into the stream. Captain Vyner was one of the first to get his head out of the water and to save himself from the current by clinging to the upturned vessel. After a hard struggle he reached the top of the boat and was able to assist first Sir George Wombwell and afterwards one of the York officers to the top of the boat. Mr White got on shore by clinging to the chain stretched across the ferry. Sir Charles struck out, some say for the further shore, some say for the upturned boat. His horse, seeing his master, swam after him and it seemed as if Sir Charles might be dragged to safety. But Sir Charles grabbed the bridle and both horse and master sank into the river. In a brief space of time it was all over.

Six of those who had boarded the ferry were missing. Mr Lloyd, who was a good swimmer, had been seen to strike out strongly but he had made for the bank that was farthest away and he failed to reach it. Mr Robinson, who could not swim, had stayed on his horse. He remained calm as the horse swam towards the banking but as the horse began to sink he panicked, screaming for help. Orvis and the ferrymen were the others missing and as they had not been seen after the boat capsized it was assumed that they must have been unable to escape from beneath. Sir George Wombwell was almost insensible when Captain Vyner got him onto the boat and he said later that he was so exhausted that he couldn't remember how he was saved. Major Mussenden of the 8th Hussars was badly kicked by the horses whilst under water and others sustained injuries of similar character.

Many of the rescuers themselves had narrow escapes. Ingilby of Ripley Castle, Richard Thompson of Kirby Hall and Robert Vyner were all nearly drowned in their efforts to save Lloyd and Sir Charles.

By late on Thursday night only three of the missing bodies had been recovered. Sir Charles' corpse was found about half-past four, about 300 yards below where the accident happened and close to a small waterfall. The bodies of Mr Lloyd and Mr Robinson were recovered soon afterwards near to the same spot. Mr Robinson's watch had stopped at ten minutes to two o'clock, which was when the accident happened.

Again, stories differ about the survival of the horses. Some state that only one horse survived, some that *Old Saltfish* was found lying dead beside his master but most eyewitness accounts suggest that the horse scrambled out of the river further up the banking and was later taken back to his stable. Many of the other poor beasts drowned, thanks to the folly of their riders.

On Friday an inquest into the deaths of five of the drowned men, was held in the dining room of Newby Hall and a verdict of accidental death was recorded.

On Monday, William Tempest, a police constable in the West Riding force stationed at Copt Hewick, discovered the body of James Warriner, about 25

St John's Church, Knaresborough

yards below the ferry. The body was identified by Thomas Warriner of Skelton, a gardener and James' brother. At the inquest, the main witness was Lizzie Wilkinson, daughter of James Wilkinson of Newby with Mulwith, who was also a gardener. She confirmed that she knew James, describing the events: 'I never saw James Warriner alive again,' she said.

Mr Robinson was said to have been one of the best riders in the county, whilst William Orvis had worked with the York and Ainsty hounds for many years and was one of the most experienced whips in Yorkshire, though he was actually born in Norfolk. He had two young daughters.

Both the Warriners were married – one left nine children, the other a wife and three children.

Sir Charles, who was unmarried, was the tenth Baron Slingsby, and a very popular man; a staunch Conservative and active supporter of local candidates, as well as being a Deputy Lieutenant of Yorkshire and a local magistrate. Born in 1824, he had succeeded his uncle Thomas to the

Tomb of Sir Charles Slingsby, Knaresborough

baronetcy, but because of this accident, the baronetcy of Slingsby, which for 500 years had descended in a direct line, became extinct.

The body of Sir Charles was taken back to Scriven Park and placed in a thin wooden shell, which was then put into a lead coffin. The whole was then put into a coffin of polished oak.

Exactly a week after the accident, Knaresborough closed all its shops. The streets were lined with mourners as the funeral procession of Sir Charles Slingsby made its slow way from his home to his last resting place in a new vault in the Slingsby Chapel in St John's Church. A special train had to be put on to take friends and acquaintances to and from York and all hunting was stopped throughout the country as a mark of respect.

Just a few days later, on 23 February, Sir George Wombwell was voted in as master of the York and Ainsty Hunt.

A poem was written in memory of the event, describing the huntsmen, the long run over rough country and the final embarkation onto the ferryboat. The final stanza reads:

Though bravest man tried man to save,
'Twas not to be: the greedy wave
Two friends devoured, a servant true,
Two boatmen strong – that vessel's crew.
    The rescuer's arm,
    The rope of thongs,
    Mid all the harm
    One life prolongs.
Forget not ye, who saw and live –
Remember WHO can take and give.
Hall, cottage, stall, some coming day
For thee shall, echoing empty, say,
'Gone away!'

The victims:
Sir Charles Slingsby, Bart, of Scriven Park
Mr E Lloyd, of Lingcroft, near York
Mr Edmund Robinson, of York
William Orvis, first whip
C Warriner, gardener at Newby Hall
James Warriner, son of the above

Sources:
North Yorkshire Record Office – Inquest on James Warriner C4/3 1869
West Yorkshire Archives Service, Leeds – WYL230/3579
Huddersfield Daily Examiner 1869
The Annals of Yorkshire – John Mayhall

9

Fire at St John's Church

Wortley, Leeds

1891

Asale of work to raise funds for the local church was a regular occurrence in most English parishes in the nineteenth century. St John's church, Wortley, in Leeds was no exception, but in 1891 the plans were a little more extensive. Eleanor Coleman, a young seventeen-year-old who lived nearby in Thornhill Road where she worked for Mrs J R Steele, suggested a performance known as 'Snowflakes'. The same entertainment had been performed in various other churches in the district previously, with the girls dressed appropriately in cotton dresses, over which cotton wool had been fluffed up and stitched in a semblance of snow. A Band of Hope member, Eli Auty, agreed to the idea and rehearsals began, though Eleanor's employer soon told her there was too much work to do elsewhere for her to continue. Auty however carried on, helped by Charles Clegg, a local warehouseman. The excited children quickly got permission to take part from their parents and friends rallied round to make the required costumes.

On New Year's Eve the first show was put on for the parents and friends in the area. The little girls clambered up on to the temporary platform which had been built at one end of the school room, trooped out of the cramped dressing room to the room set aside for the entertainment and dutifully performed their songs. All went well and

SHOCKING AFFAIR IN LEEDS.

FIRE AT AN ENTERTAINMENT.

FOURTEEN CHILDREN IN FLAMES.

One of those disasters which are especially harrowing

Headline, Yorkshire Post

everyone looked forward to a repeat performance the following night.

On Thursday, New Year's Day of 1891, things were running a little late. Perhaps the girls were over excited by their success on Wednesday and it seemed to take longer to get them organised and dressed. Mrs Dixon and some of the mothers finally succeeded in getting them into their costumes and left the dressing room, which was already crowded with children, benches, chairs and other furniture. Mr Auty, who was one of the men in charge of the entertainment, lined the troupe up. To get onto the stage they had to climb onto a chair and then onto the platform, but at the same time the girls had to carry a Chinese paper lantern. Inside the lantern was a lighted candle, but the girls had been given strict instructions to take care and:

> 'that if any accident did take place with the lanterns they were to throw them straight before them towards the audience and not allow the light to get near their own dresses'.

So with these safety procedures in place, the entertainment was ready to start. No one was quite sure what happened next but according to Mr Auty, the only adult present in the room:

> 'We had,' he says, 'formed the girls in order ready to step upon the platform in the adjoining room. We had lighted thirteen of the fourteen lanterns and were about to illuminate the last one, when a spark fell upon the cotton wool jacket of Emily Tyner. In an instant, before I could do anything she was enveloped in flames, which I endeavoured to extinguish by taking her up in my arms. What occurred immediately after I cannot say definitely; all I can say is that the next moment the whole of the fourteen children without exception were in a mass of flame. My theory as to the rapid spread of the fire is this; one of the girls was holding a naked light for me while I lit the lanterns and I am afraid that in her terror she rushed towards the door with the light and stumbling over the other girls, set them all ablaze. It was the work of an instant.'

Osborne Taylor, forge man, father of Alice Taylor who was also taking part, had gone on Thursday night to see the entertainment but as he went in he saw a child with her clothing on fire trying to climb over a seat. Suddenly all the girls seemed to be on fire. He rushed into the middle of them, but the smoke was so thick that he broke a window to let in some fresh air, which may have made the situation even worse. He then did his best to put out the flames on the girls, pulling off the wool on their clothes. They surround him with the burning material and in the general din and confusion he was unable to recognise his own daughter till she called out to him: 'Father, come to me!' He went to her and put out the flames as well as he was able but she was later taken to the infirmary with serious burns

The vicar (Canon Brameld) and the curate (Rev E F Buckton) along with many others grabbed coats and rugs, wrapping them round the girls in an attempt to put out the flames. Police, fire brigade and ambulance were soon on the spot and twelve of the fifteen girls were taken to the Leeds Infirmary. Two others were treated at home by local doctors. Only one girl escaped without injury.

Initially the report in the paper named the twelve girls, and gave their injuries as not particularly serious, but eventually this proved wrong. The girls were:

Caroline Eveline Steel, nine, Vine Cottage, Thornhill Road, Wortley.

Alice Taylor, fourteen, daughter of Osborne Taylor, Western Street, Low Wortley.

Elizabeth Tingle, twelve, daughter of Benjamin Tingle, Greenside Road, Low Wortley.

Clarissa Roberts, eleven, daughter of Joseph Roberts, Albany Street, Sliver Royd Hill, Upper Wortley.

Harriet Riley, twelve, daughter of Eliza Riley, Greenhill, Wortley.

Miriam Stokes, sixteen, daughter of John Thomas Stokes, Western View, Town End, Low Wortley.

Emily Tyner, nine, daughter of James Tyner, Western View, Town End, Low Wortley.

Sarah Ellen Kitchen, fourteen, daughter of Tom Atha Kitchen, Scarborough Villa, Waingate, Armley.

Maggie Kitchen, twelve, sister of the above.

Ada Whittron, eleven, living with David Whittron, her uncle, at Bowling Garth Terrace, Upper Wortley.

Emily Lister, thirteen, daughter of John Lister, Cabbage Hill, Upper Wortley.

Ethel Fieldhouse, fourteen, daughter of W Fieldhouse, Fawcett Lane, Lower Wortley.

Besides the twelve children who were taken to the infirmary, others included Julia Florence Anderson, Emily Sanderson and Florrie Brookes, sister of the caretaker. These were carried to their homes as their injuries were thought not serious. Among other people burnt besides the girls were Osborne Taylor, Charles Clayton, warehouseman, Weston Grove, Wortley; Charles Clegg of Wortley and Eli Auty. None of these had serious injuries.

Over the next few days, one after another of the girls died, not just from their burns but from shock. Emily Lister was the first to succumb,

Leeds Old Infirmary

followed by Caroline Steel, Clarissa Roberts, Ethel Fieldhouse and Maggie Kitchen all within a few hours of each other. Ada Whittron died next, whilst Florrie Brookes, who had been taken home as doctors thought she was not too badly hurt, died shortly afterwards. Elizabeth Tingle and Harriet Riley died on 8 January, soon followed by Emily Sanderson and Julia Florence Anderson.

The *Yorkshire Post* described the harrowing scenes at the hospital, particularly once it was realised that many of the children would not survive:

'... the final interviews which parents and friends had with the delirious, expiring little sufferers were too heartrending, too sacred almost, to be written about. But what transpired at those bedside farewells was not nearly so pathetic as an episode that, at midnight, moved to the quick the most cool and clear-headed of nurses and doctors. Three or four of the pretty little folk who were more seriously burnt than their playmates were put together in the accident ward. When they had laid there for a couple of hours or so the numbness of delirium deadened their sense of pain, and all the three or four dreadfully-scorched victims hummed snatches of the solos, duets, trios and choruses that they were to

have sung in their schoolroom. Only the nurses, whose loving care cannot be over-praised, lingered within earshot of these musical meanderings of the three or four bonny little lasses, every one of whom had passed away before noon yesterday.'

The newspaper commented:

'In the last twenty-four hours the gruesomeness of this New Year's Day's tragedy has deepened – deepened as one after one of the young victims has closed her eyes in her last sleep, and so ended her terrible sufferings and deepened as the mind has had more time to grasp hold of all the details of the calamity.'

An inquest was soon arranged, opened by J C Malcolm (Borough Coroner) at Leeds Town Hall. The jury initially went to view the bodies as usual before attempting to listen to the evidence. The coroner was accompanied on the bench by the Mayor (Alf Cooke) and the Town Clerk (Sir George Morrison) and in the body of the court were the Rev Dr Talbot, vicar of Leeds, the Rev Canon Brameld, vicar, and the Rev E F Buckton, curate of St John's, Upper Wortley; Councillors Battle and Goodson, ex-Councillor Kettlewell, C C Joliffe (Deputy Town Clerk) and John Thornton (Magistrate's Clerk). The Chief Constable, F T Webb, watched the inquiry on behalf of the police. The inquest had to be adjourned on numerous occasions to allow time for those injured to recover sufficiently to attend but gradually the story was put together.

In his initial opening remarks the coroner spoke to the jury:

'If what has appeared in the newspapers this morning may be taken as a criterion of what has happened, we must be inclined to think that there has been a maximum amount of danger. The children appear to have been clothed in very inflammable material – cotton wool – and altogether the circumstances are such as will necessitate a full and adequate inquiry in order to ascertain if there has been fault or relaxation of duty on the part of anyone. Those entrusted with the care of the children have had a great responsibility thrown upon them and it will be necessary to ascertain if they took every proper means for the safety of the children of such tender years that had been entrusted to them. That is the principal part of the inquiry.'

B G A Moynihan, the surgeon from the hospital, was first asked how the girls died, confirming that they all died from severe burns and shock. The coroner then turned his attention to the room in which the entertainment had taken place. Was it actually licensed for such an event?

John Thornton, Clerk to the Justices for the Borough of Leeds, produced a register of licences up to end 1890. A licence had been granted to Rev John Trower in June 1889 which expired at the end of 1889. There was no record of any application being made for a renewal of the licence at the beginning of 1890 and therefore the licence had lapsed.

Walter Yates, Committee clerk of the Leeds Corporation, gave evidence to the effect that there had been no application for a licence for the St John's School, Wortley to the Corporation since the duty of granting such licences was transferred from the justices to the Corporation.

A copy of the minutes of the Watch Committee was read out to the effect that a question had arisen regarding the recent action of the police with reference to the licensing of Sunday school occasionally used for entertainment. It was decided that the Chief Constable be instructed not to prosecute such cases in future.

However, it was also established that when an application was made for special licenses the committee would have made inquires about the rooms, checked exits and other matters in order to check whether a licence was needed and whether it was advisable to grant it. In the case at St John's church no such visit had been made.

Canon Brameld was questioned closely about his knowledge of the event. The Band of Hope had asked to have the entertainment but no one had actually asked them what it was. The title 'Snowflakes' appeared in the programme and it was known that a number of young children would take part but no one on the organising committee really knew what was going on. They just left it to the Band of Hope organisers – Eli Auty and Charles Clegg.

Clegg confirmed that he had been involved but 'didn't have much to do with it,' he said, just conducted the singing but he was questioned about any apparent danger:

> *'When you were preparing the entertainment did any one tell you it was dangerous?'*
> *'No, all the jackets were made to fit, I think. The wool did not appear fluffy. It was not the common kind of cotton wool, it seemed to be the best kind. The wool was teased out to make it as right as possible.'*
> *'Was the other part of the children's dresses composed of cotton wool?'*
> *'Yes.'*
> *'Were the lamps knocking one against the other?'*
> *'We cautioned them about that.'*
> *'Had you seen the lamps striking each other?'*
> *'I do not remember seeing them.'*

'Then why did you caution them?'
'We had a practice on Saturday night and sometimes the children forgot and put the lanterns nearly to one another and we naturally told them they must look to their lanterns and keep them off one another.'
The coroner replied:
'On Saturday night the lanterns were not lighted – there was no necessity to caution them.'

The organisers still denied that they had seen any danger, though the lanterns had been mounted on to sticks to make them 'safe'. Eleanor Coleman, who had first suggested the idea, described in her evidence how the lanterns should have been dealt with:

'A long stick and hold the lanterns away from us and a bigger platform. The lanterns should be fixed on the top of the sticks with thicker wire so that there was no swaying.'

'Did you explain about the lanterns to either Mr Auty or Mr Clegg?'

'No.'

Eventually, Eli Auty, who had also been taken to the infirmary for treatment, was well enough to take the stand. He was able to add to his earlier comments about the events:

'I tried, first with one girl then with another, to put out the fire and then made for the doorway leading on to the temporary platform or stage in the hope that I might help them escape by that, the only exit. Unfortunately, however, the chair which was to be used for enabling the girls to get upon the platform was not there and being small children they were unable to climb upon the stage. Thereupon I, getting upon the platform, endeavoured to lift them up with the object of passing them on to the people who were waiting to take charge of them, but the cotton wool in which they were clothed parted from the lining of their dress whenever I tried to lift them and every time they slipped out of my hands. Failing in this I went back into the dressing room and again did my best to quench the flames in which the young children were enveloped.'

He told the court that he had no thought of danger. The coroner queried this:

'Neither as to the crowding in the room, the getting on and off the stage, nor anything connected with the lights?'

'No.'

The police were asked about both the dressing room and the room with the platform stage. All was confusion when they arrived but examination proved that:

> 'The door leading to the yard was locked and bolted and the only exit was across the platform into the entertainment room.'

The dressing room, which was 16 feet 5 inches long and 21 feet 3 inches wide, had housed chairs, benches and other furniture as well as being the room where fourteen excited little girls were getting changed and expected to carry lighted paper lanterns. The only exit from this room had to be reached by climbing onto a platform 2 feet 7 inches high and through a door only 2 feet 2 inches wide.

Fanny Amelia Craven, the fourteen-year-old daughter of Wilson Craven, of Greenside Road, had been asked to play the music for the girls. She and her sister, Phoebe, who was helping her, were the only children to survive with no injuries. She was in the class room whilst the children were dressing and Mrs Dixon, Mrs Roberts, Mr Auty and Mr Clegg were there assisting. She was asked:

> 'Did you see any of the lanterns lighted that night?'

> 'Yes and I heard Mr Auty tell them to be careful and not let the lanterns go against one another. I was late on Thursday and the girls were nearly ready when I got to the room. I had no dress to put on. I saw the lanterns lighted by Mr Auty – I think with a match. There was no lighted candle. The children were standing there holding lanterns.'

She then went onto stage, preparing her music when she heard and saw a blaze in the door way. She admitted that she had found it difficult to get up onto the platform which was too high, even though she was unencumbered by anything, let alone a lighted lantern.

Again the jury wanted to know the details:

> 'Did Mr Auty help the children on the stage the first night?'
> 'I did not see, I don't think so.'
> 'Did you see the children come on to the stage the first night with the lanterns?'
> 'Yes.'
> 'Did they look at all awkward on coming on to the stage in that way?'

'They did look awkward. I did not see anyone by the side of the stage to help the children on. I was on the stage.'

Fanny was not the only one with disconcerting evidence. When Mrs Inman, the mother of one of the injured children, appeared she stated that, not only were the lanterns being lit but: 'There was a fire in the room and no guard in front.' The jury began to wonder whether this could also have contributed to the fire.

Edward Ward, one of the surgeons at the Leeds Infirmary who was in charge of all the children admitted to hospital confirmed to the court that cotton wadding was very inflammable anyway but when teased out to look 'fluffy' it is even more so. He produced some cotton wool and set fire to it to demonstrate how quickly it would blaze. The jury was in no doubt about the speed with which the catastrophe took place, but they were still not sure who to blame. The church committee was questioned again.

John Russell Williams, manager, Nan Tan House, Upper Wortley, who was on the general committee said that no one had suggested to him that children should be dressed up in this way. He had only found out on the night of the first performance since he had not had a programme and didn't ask what they were going to do, just knew they were going to provide some entertainment. He did not see any danger, didn't think the stage was crowded, didn't know the number who were going to perform, but felt his responsibility was for the tableaux and theatricals and therefore knew nothing about the children's entertainment.

Canon Brameld again had to provide an explanation:

'I should not have permitted it if I had known what it was going to be. I did not see the lighted lamps at all on the first night. I was not in. I saw two lamps lighted on the second night – the night of the catastrophe – and if I had known the lamps were to be lighted I should have forbidden the whole thing. … It never occurred to me that these were cotton wool dresses. I knew the danger of cotton wool. I was so busy over other things that I went off without thinking of the danger.'

He also suggested that Auty and Clegg had volunteered to act as a sub-committee, but when the minutes of the church committee were read out, there was no reference to 'Snowflakes'.

The coroner was somewhat scathing:

'It may be said, Canon Brameld, that you, as head of the church, are primarily responsible for all the arrangements and it should be explained how it is that two gentlemen like Mr Auty and Mr Clegg could bring about

an entertainment which is now proved to be dangerous without having your
approval or the approval of the members of the committee.'

Brameld immediately defended his fellow committee members, stating that
no one else had any responsibility for the event: 'they never heard a word
about it'.

The coroner was having none of it:

'*But as members of the committee, they should have done... it is strange and*
requires explanation, how such a dangerous exhibition could have been put
upon the stage in your schoolroom without you having permitted it or the
committee sanctioned it.'

As the evidence came to an end the coroner addressed the jury:

'*This is a case of great public importance and the jury's difficulty would be*
to lay aside as far as possible all feelings of bias. They would have to decide
whether this accident was caused by some means which ordinary care and
forethought could not have provided against or whether there had been any
negligence. Dealing with the legal aspect of the question in respect to the
licensing of the room he showed that the committee were not in error on this
point and with regard to the entertainment itself that there was no illegal act
committed inasmuch as the children were not performing for their own
profit.'

Later he said that 'acts of omission should be taken into account as much as
those of commission' referring particularly to the fact that none of the
members of the committee had any knowledge of the nature of the entertainment prior to its performance. However, the committee had no specific legal
responsibility for the children. The matter was therefore narrowed down to
the question of the liability of Auty, the man who had suffered terribly from
his injuries and they had to consider whether there was any act on his part
which rendered him responsible because it was during his manipulation of
the lanterns that the accident occurred. If whilst he was performing a legal
act, he was so careless that lives were placed in danger he would be
responsible.

Fifty-five minutes later the jury returned to court with a written verdict:

'*We find that the cause of death was shock to the system from burns caused*
by deceased's clothing taking fire at an entertainment at the school room of
St John's Upper Wortley...
  That the clothing of the children for that entertainment was of a most

dangerous material; that the danger was greatly increased by supplying the children with lights; that the arrangements were such as to further increase the danger by having an unguarded fire in the dressing room, by the crowded state of that room, with benches, chairs and other furniture, the difficult means of access for the children to and from the stage and the want of space on the stage for such an entertainment; the immediate cause of the fire being the ignition of a lantern which set fire to the clothing of one of the children, the fire spreading among the others whilst crowding in the doorway leading to the stage and that the ignition of such lantern was accidental, though brought about by carrying lights whilst enveloped in such combustible material in a crowded room and by children of tender age, having no conception of the danger they were incurring.

We further find that the Rev Canon Brameld, the Rev E F Buckton and Mr J R Willans, as the members of the committee for the sale of work accepted a duty and responsibility as to all the arrangements and entertainment concerned therewith as announced in the programme and that they have not exercised such forethought, care and supervision as such duty imposed upon them. Though finding a verdict of accidental death, we find there has been great negligence on their part. We also find there was negligence on the part of Mr Auty and Mr Clegg who had accepted the special care of the children and we are not satisfied with the manner and truthfulness of the evidence of Mr Clegg.

We recommend that the Licensing Authority should consider the advisability of withdrawing the resolution as to the free use of schoolrooms for such entertainments, in order that the provision may be made in licenses for protection of the public as on other licensed premises and especially with a view to safeguard children of tender age whose services are used for attracting audiences.

We desire to express our admiration of the conduct of the vicar and others who were present and assisted in the rescue and removal of the children and particularly of the conduct of Mr Auty in the trying and dangerous position in which he was placed and we tender our sympathy with them and the parents of the children in their distress.'

Caroline Eveline Steel and Maggie Kitchen were buried at St John's church close by the school. The coffins were brought from the homes of the parents to the entrance of the churchyard and then carried by friends from the Sunday school. Carrie Steel's parents and grandparents, Mr and Mrs W Watson, were there along with her sister Emily, brother Willie and other relatives, as were the parents of Maggie Kitchen and her brothers, Robert and Willie and sisters, Laura and Jeannie. Maggie's grandparents, Mr and Mrs Peter Kitchen, were the first couple married in the church over fifty years previously.

St John's Church, Wortley

When Ethel Fieldhouse was buried, her school friends carried her coffin, each carrying a little bouquet to throw into the grave. As well as wreaths from her parents, three brothers and three sisters, there was a small wreath from Miss Turner, Sunday school teacher. Sunday school teachers, Miss Sugden and Miss Walker and scholars of the adult class carried Emily Lister's coffin.

Superintendent Dalton and a staff of constables were present both at the church and at the cemetery as representatives of the local police force and:

'at the latter place succeeded in arresting a pickpocket who had not hesitated to carry on his nefarious calling at the graveside and who is believed to have stolen a woman's purse, at Oldfield Lane Cemetery'.

After the funeral of all the children a Relief Fund was set up and eventually a memorial stone erected in the churchyard inscribed with all their names and dedicated to:

'Eleven children who lost their lives through accident by fire in Wortley Church Hall on New Year's Day.'

Source:
Yorkshire Evening Post 1891

Memorial stone, St John's churchyard

10

Public Hall Disaster

Barnsley

1908

In January 1908 the Harvey Institute, generally known as the Public Hall, in Barnsley, was rented by the World's Cinematograph Company where they held a series of matinee and evening performances of the new media of film – an exciting and novel experience for many.

On Saturday 11 January the price of admission was reduced to just one penny (less than half a modern day penny) that brought the show within the reach of the less well off – and children. The gallery had seating for only about 400 adults, yet over 600 children were sold tickets and still more were queuing outside. George Burkinshaw, the caretaker of the hall, informed the Company that the gallery was as full as he considered to be safe and that no more should be admitted. The box office were told and confirmed that they were no longer selling seats there.

Outside in the yard the queue of children seemed just as long as when the doors first opened. A new doorman, Gray, was supposed to be controlling the children but simply allowed them inside in batches of a dozen or more at a time. Mr Rain, at the top of the stairs, took the pennies and shepherded them into the gallery. The stairs twisted and turned on their way upward, taking the children out of sight of the two men for much of the time.

Burkinshaw went back to the balcony, which was just below the gallery, preparing to watch the show. He sat, watching the children filing in, then noticed that the doorman in the gallery was beckoning him. 'Tell them to come,' he called down, 'the children are falling down the steps.'

The children climbing the steps had been told that they must turn back and they would be admitted to the seats lower down in the hall. Eager to reach the better seats, the children

Headline, Barnsley Chronicle

turned and tried to push their way down. Unfortunately, those lower down had no idea what was happening, so continued trying to go up to the gallery. As the two streams met, inevitably a 'jam' occurred and panic ensued.

Children at the bottom of the staircase fell, or perhaps were pushed over by those above, others fell on top, crushing those below them, only to be crushed in their turn. Some of the children rushed out into the yard, screaming that their brothers or sisters were fallen. Burkinshaw rushed to their assistance, going round to the gallery entrance in the yard. Realising that he could not cope alone he went for help, calling on men such as William Robinson and Joseph Wilson from Porter's Warehouse nearby. Police and fire brigade were called and fortunately William Batley, in charge of the borough ambulance service, was in the area, giving immediate aid and supervising the transport of children to the hospital. Quickly the uninjured children were helped to safety and the injured were transported to Beckett Hospital. Most were allowed home within a few hours, though a few were more serious and had to remain. The dead were gently laid out on straw in the yard, before being moved to the mortuary at the hospital.

Two of the little girls were taken to Dr John Hall, whose surgery was close by, but Flossie Smith died on the journey. Annie Lee was treated there for a while before being taken to the hospital, whilst both Dr Hall and his wife ran to help at the scene of the crisis.

The manager of the Company, Mr Atroy, had been in the main entrance when the accident happened. He ordered the film to start immediately in an attempt to keep the other children in their seats and calm. Once he found out what had happened he went on the stage, informed the audience that there 'had been an accident' and that the performance would not continue, asking them to file out quietly and calmly.

Many older children were sent in charge of younger siblings or neighbours' children.

Walter McGrath, twelve, was at the show with his friend, Fred Swift. They were both in charge of younger children – Walter brought a neighbour's son, six-year-old Willie Senior and Swift brought his little sister, Nellie, also six and younger brother Leonard. At the entrance, Leonard turned back, saying it was too crowded and went off to spend his money on chocolate. The others stayed, slowly moving upwards on the stair, Walter telling young Willie to hang on tight to the iron railing. As the crisis began and children began falling, he called out again to the lad: 'Don't leave go of the iron.' Walter was knocked down on top of other children and fainted but woke later to find that others were pressing down on top of him and he couldn't move. Finally he managed to crawl out, clutching at other children to haul himself upright. Walking home he discovered that, though his friend had got out, Nellie Swift was killed. Willie had listened to the older boy's advice, hung on to the rails and not even been knocked down.

Beatrice Cartwright, seven, was sent with Lucy Beevers who was twelve. Though they tried hard not to be separated, in the crush their hands parted and, later, Lucy had the distressing experience of finding Beatrice's body lying dead in the straw in the yard before removal to the mortuary.

The Jackson family were much luckier. Jenny Jackson, twelve, had taken her younger brothers, four-year-old Ronald and nine-year-old Harold as well as her sister Clara, six. It was impossible for her to hold on to all of them and eventually lost touch with Clara. As the stream of children tried to drag themselves to safety, Jenny managed to grab the little girl again, hauling the two younger children out into the yard. Once there, she discovered that she had actually grabbed a neighbour's child, Maud Taylor, who was unconscious. Thankfully, Clara did eventually get out and the whole family were able to return home together.

Thomas Lee 'a fine strapping lad' of fifteen took his little sister, Mary, who was five. Realising what was happening, he picked her up and tried to escape but fell, trapping the child beneath him. Despite his best efforts to save her, no one was able to pull the little girl out in time. Most of the children died through suffocation, wedged in so tight their rescuers couldn't drag them out.

Charles Plumpton, editor of the *Barnsley Chronicle*, explained how anxious relatives arriving and trying to find their children hampered rescue efforts. Even men from the pit, still in their working clothes, were seen crying at the horror of the situation.

The funerals took place in the local cemetery, which was closed to the public to give the families privacy, but thousands lined the streets nearby to express their sympathy and sorrow at the event. Parents and friends carried the little coffins – those of Hardy and Mary Stott being carried by their friends – four boys and four girls respectively. A relief fund was opened for a few days but 'sufficient contributions to meet all needs' were quickly received.

The inquest was quickly opened, presided over by Mr Maitland at the Town Hall, with a local jury. Four of these refused to swear an oath – Brady Webster (who was later chosen as foreman) and W E Brady, because they were Quakers. The other two, Mr Vaine and E G Bayford, 'for other reasons'. All were allowed to 'affirm' instead and the inquest was able to proceed. Either father or mother of each of the dead children had to come forward and give evidence of identification when 'even the fathers broke down in telling about the identification of their bairns – as for the mothers, hardly a word could be heard of their dispositions owing to their great emotion.' Henry Watson, a labourer, of Tower Street, stated that he was the adoptive father of Florence May Smith whom he had adopted when she was only eight months old. Her real father was Wilfred Smith, a blacksmith, of Greenwood Terrace. Every parent was asked by the coroner: 'Was your child insured?' and invariably the answer given was: 'Yes, sir.'

Even more heart rending was the evidence of Mrs Graham. She came to identify her son, John, and when asked why she was there instead of her husband, had to say that her husband had died that morning of heart disease, intensified by the loss of their child.

Whilst there were a number of criticisms raised, such as the need for more attendants at each turn of the staircase and greater control of the crowds of children, the jury decided that the organisers of the event were simply 'negligent' in not providing proper supervision, not 'criminally negligent' so no further proceedings were taken. The coroner also pointed out that it 'was not wise' for parents to send small children to such events in the charge only of an older brother or sister.

Many poems were written about the event. This appeared in the *Barnsley Chronicle* just few days after the disaster:

In Memoriam
Hush'd are the children's voices
We heard but yesterday
And hush'd the merry laughter
Oft echoing light and gay.

The little footstep patter
The loving baby smile
Have vanished in a moment
And so we weep awhile.

But lo! From highest Heaven
With peace no words can tell
A Voice comes
through the darkness,
I took them – all is well. (Alfred E Lean FRGS)

Those who died:
Harry Williams, six, Victor Terrace
Alice Marshall, four, Albion Terrace
John Charles Hibbert, five, Tower Street
Florence May (Flossie) Smith, eight, Tower Street
Mary Lee, five, Castlereagh Street
William Parkin Goodall, six, Beech Street
Annie Johnson, four, Commercial Street
Hardy Stott, four, Heelis Street
Mary E Stott, eight, Heelis Street
Ellen Swift, six, Beech Street

Edward Pickles, eight, Wortley Street
Beatrice Cartwright, seven, King Street
Albert Ward, five, Manor Castle Yard
John Charles Graham, eight, Mill Street
Winnie Cousins, seven, Sovereign Yard
Charlotte Norton, six, Cope Street

From *Supplement to Lloyds News 1908:*

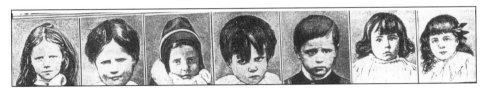

Extract from Lloyds News

Mary Stott, Ellen Swift, Beatrice Cartwright, Hardy Stott, John Graham, Annie Johnson, Charlotte Whitworth

Extract from Lloyds News

Harry Williams, Winnie Cousins, John C Hibbert, Mary Lee, William Goodall, Alice Marshall

Injured who were treated at hospital:
Willie Johnson, Garden Street; John Booth, Wakefield Road; Annie Lee, Oxford Street; Annie Vickers, Lister Square; Lucy Beevers, King Street; Alethea Marfleet, Doncaster Road; Henry (or Harry) Jackson, Grace Street; Doris Pickering, Seth Terrace; Maud Taylor, Cope Street; Clara Jackson, Duke Street; Ben Lowe, Heelis Street; Annie Jackson, King Street; Ivy Baker, High Street, Worsbrough.

Source:
Barnsley Chronicle 1908

On 13 January 2008, one hundred years after the event, a memorial service, which included some of the descendents of survivors, was held and a plaque, commemorating the children who died, placed at the site of the disaster.

11

Charabanc Accident

Oxenhope, Keighley

1920

At 12.25pm on Saturday 31 October 1920 a group of thirty-two people set off in a charabanc from the *Robin Hood's Inn*, Pecket Well near Hebden Bridge. The excuse was a knurr and spell match at Colne in which the men were competing, but the women were just going for the ride and to look at the shops. All, including the landlord who was going too, were in a holiday mood and ready for an enjoyable day's trip. Following behind them were other charabancs in which were the Hebden Bridge Male Voice Choir and their friends.

Robin Hood's Inn, Pecket Well

The charabanc set off over Cockhill Moor on its way towards Oxenhope and Keighley. There is a steady decline for about two miles and at the bottom just before coming into Oxenhope there is a dangerous left hand bend in the road.

About a quarter of a mile or so from the bend the driver of the charabanc started to apply the brakes. Nothing happened. The brakes had failed and the charabanc quickly got out of control, gathering speed as it rushed downhill.

On rounding the bend it ran right across the road and crashed into a stone wall, tearing down about twenty yards of it. The rear of the charabanc sprang up and the vehicle would have overturned but it hit a large tree on the right hand side and fell back again.

The landlord of the *Robin Hood's Inn*, John Murgatroyd later said:

> *'As we approached the end I shut my eyes and awaited the crash. It was a fearful shock. The charabanc, which was very badly damaged, belongs to Messrs Greenhaugh & Shaw of Rochdale. All the doors on one side were ripped off and the front of the car smashed. The driver was Tom Hey who lives at Holesworth Street, Rochdale. He did his utmost to avoid the smash. He escaped with nothing more serious than cuts on the hands. When the crash came, nearly all the passengers were pitched out but one or two at the front managed to retain their places in the vehicle. On the front seat, in addition to the driver were William Henry Greenwood and Thomas Greenwood. The driver, who had still hold of the steering wheel, was not thrown out, neither was Thomas Greenwood who had hold of the front rail. Greenwood was thrown violently against the rail fracturing his ribs. John Graham who was sitting in an outside seat near the centre of the charabanc was flung out and landed on top of a small wooden hut, which was damaged by the charabanc. Some of the other passengers were thrown a distance of several yards.'*

One of the group realised early what was happening and jumped out of the back of the charabanc before the crash came. William Hartley was a keen motorcyclist so knew quite a lot about engines. He felt the brakes give way. '... and I went with them d...d soon afterwards', he said later.

Hartley was in the back seat and that seat was the one, with its occupants, to suffer the most. The

MOORLAND CHARA TRAGEDY

Graphic Story of Oxenhope Disaster.

WHOLE VILLAGE PLUNGED INTO MOURNING.

Interviews with Survivors.

Headline, Halifax Courier

two other people sitting in it were killed, but Hartley merely cut himself severely on the hand by dropping out. Without pausing to look at the disaster, he dashed straight past on his way for help, making a trail of dripping blood from his injured hand.

He had not gone very far when he met a constable who was so shocked by his appearance that it took a moment before he realised what had happened. Then, before the lad could tell his story, another of the injured came along the road with bleeding head and the constable needed no further information. He started to organise help and told Hartley where to go in the village. Luckily the village doctor was coming along the road at the time and as soon as he realised what had happened, he dashed off at once to the scene of the disaster.

The other charabancs that had been following, were directed to go straight on into Keighley to arrange for further help and to alert the hospital, which immediately sent its ambulance. The local newspapers were graphic in their description:

> 'It was a terrible scene with blood for a background. The brains of one of the victims were found to have been dashed right out and stuck against a tree.'

As always though rumour spread quickly. It was said that the victims numbered twenty injured and ten killed but it was soon discovered that the actual figure was not so high.

Those who died included:

William Kershaw, thirty-five, a mason's labourer, Keighley Road, Pecket Well, near Hebden Bridge and his wife Alice. Alice had been ill and this was her first day out of doors. William was a reservist at the outbreak of war, and was in the retreat from Mons with the Irish Rifles being later wounded and discharged. The family were no strangers to death, this being the fifth death since 1917. Mr Fletcher, Alice's father, died in 1918, one brother died as a prisoner in Germany in 1918 and husband of another Fletcher daughter, Nurse Pickwell, of the Lying in Charity, Hull, was killed in France.

John Turner, mason's labourer, Waterloo Bank, Wadsworth. He was forty-two, leaving a widow and six children of whom the youngest was only three years old. His widow suffered very badly from a heart condition and was not fit to go to the hospital to claim her husband. Even his dog knew something was wrong, refusing to go into the house and moping about generally in the road outside.

William Ogden, a fifty-six-year-old mill hand, of Ivy Cottage, Pecket Well. He had served for twelve years on the committee of the local Co-operative stores, and was very well liked in the village.

Percy Roe, thirty, warehouseman, Hebden View, Wadsworth, was a Mons medallist, serving in the Durham Light Infantry all through the war. Mr Howarth, manager of the tailoring department of the Hebden Bridge Co-operative Society, said the man had been in great spirits before the tragic outing. He had just bought a new suit to wear for the first time on this memorable occasion.

Kershaw, Turner, Ogden and Roe all worked at the local Acre Mill.

Amongst the injured were: William Henry Greenwood, a forty-seven-year-old dyer's labourer, Club Houses, Old Town, Wadsworth, with injuries to head and chest;

Thomas Greenwood, fifty-nine and a millhand, School House, Pecket Well, fractured ribs; John Graham, thirty, millhand, Chiserley Field Side, Old Town Wadsworth, fractured ribs; and Elizabeth Crosland, seventeen, also a millhand, 3 Co-op Buildings, Pecket Well, fractured pelvis

The Inquest

Police Sergeant Clarke of Haworth was the first witness called. He showed plans of the district so that the jury had some idea of the countryside in which the accident took place. From Cockhill Stoops to the scene of the accident is just over a mile, the road varying in width and gradient. The gradient from the top of the hill to the scene of the accident was one in twelve. The road surface was good. The distance from where the charabanc stopped to the scene of the accident was a little more than a mile. Here the gradient was one in fourteen.

Replying to various questions, Clarke said that the part of the road where the charabanc ought to have stopped was the steepest in the locality.

Next, James McWhirter, Keighley Road, Pecket Well, told

Gravestone, P Roe

his tale. He had been sitting in the middle seat, with Turner and Ogden. As they crossed the moor, he estimated the speed at around six or seven miles an hour but this increased to around twelve miles an hour. At the top of the hill, just before the *Wagon & Horses* pub, the driver pulled up and got under the charabanc. As he got back in he remarked 'there is a lever dropped out but it is all right now'. The jury were keen to find out if the driver had called in to the pub for a drink, which was strenuously denied by all witnesses. McWhirter then went on to comment on the driving of the bus:

> '*When we left the Robin Hood at Pecket Well about thirty yards behind he tried to get into another gear, but could not. The driver was then going uphill. It was a higher gear he wanted to get into. He could not say the reason why he could not change gear. If it had been in perfect order he would have been able to get into it.*'

Near the Oxenhope Cemetery he noticed that they were doing too much. 'I knew that there was something the matter and that there was something wrong,' he added. The driver sounded to be using the gears as a brake, which was the proper thing to do, though McWhirter could not hear whether the driver had the brakes on as well. 'He sounded to be clutching and reclutching, a thing I would not have done.' There was a bend ahead and McWhirter knew there was nothing to stop them. A passenger who was killed remarked: 'We will never do it, we will never get round the corner.' McWhirter continued:

> '*I felt a shock and felt the chassis go into the wall. I was thrown into the field at the bottom and must have turned a somersault. The shock was on the right hand corner of the chassis.*'

He confirmed that the driver did everything in his power to stop the vehicle:

> '*It was under control as far as possible... many a man would have lost his head and let it run away but he maintained control of the steering. The charabanc must have been travelling between thirty-five and forty miles an hour.*'

John Thompson-Hey of Keighley, a motor engineer, gave technical evidence arising out of an inspection of the charabanc on the morning after the accident. He said that he had applied the hand brakes and jacked up the back wheels. He could turn the wheels with a crow bar. In his opinion the brake was not efficient and would have very little power going down hill.

If either the foot brake or the sidebrake had been in proper working order the car could have been held. When asked if he would have sent out a vehicle in that state he replied, unequivocally: 'No, I would not.'

Drivers generally appear to have specific instructions about handling this type of incident. When in doubt, run into a wall!

'Our instructions in similar circumstances are that before we get right way we have to get into the wall somewhere… before we get too much speed.'

With reference to the working of the handbrake the witness said that he had not examined both rear wheels therefore he did not know whether the brake was sufficient to hold one of the wheels properly, but said that the charabanc drivers relied chiefly on their foot brakes.

Tom Hey, the driver of the charabanc, was then called and was formally cautioned. On the day in question he had no trouble between Rochdale and Pecket Well. In the journey he descended hills of a gradient similar to those at Oxenhope. He had no trouble with the brakes down those hills. The 'rack' of the hand brake was about 8 inches long, but he could only put the lever on 3 inches.

He confirmed that he did not examine the brakes, but did test them and they were keen enough. He had relined the brakes himself on 14 October. At the top of the moor, he had stopped the car because the lever of the foot accelerator slipped out. He found that there was nothing much wrong with the accelerator. Both brakes were taken off to start again. It began to gain speed about 400 yards from the scene of the accident, when the foot brake gave out. He then tried the hand brake and tried to use the engine and gears as a brake but agreed that he could not get back to low gear.

The proprietor of the charabanc had also inspected the brake. The charabanc was inspected every week. At this stage the proprietor was asked to leave the room by coroner.

After retiring for an hour and three quarters, the jury brought in a verdict of accidental death caused by injuries from being thrown out of the coach. It was noted that the brakes failed to act and the charabanc was out of control. Whilst the jury did not censure the driver they did comment that he should have engaged a lower gear. They recommended that current brakes should be made larger or more efficient and also a third emergency brake should be fitted.

T Lord, of Manchester, who was present on behalf of the owners of the charabanc, Messrs Greenhough and Shaw of Rochdale, said that he wished to state quite clearly and definitely on behalf of the owners and insurers that they admitted civil liability in connection with the accident as soon as the claims could be formulated. There seemed to be an idea in the district that each passenger was insured for a specific amount, but he told the court that it was not so.

Waingate Baptist chapel

The Funerals

All the victims were buried in Waingate Baptist Chapel in Pecket Well – William Ogden first then the remaining victims on the following Thursday. Crowds of people at the main streets of the village, blinds drawn in all the houses and business stopped in the *Robin Hood's Inn.* Many of the survivors attended. At Ogden's funeral, whilst the coffin and wreaths were brought from the house there was an intense silence. Almost all the village lined up and formed a solemn procession in front of the hearse, attended also by his widow, Edith and their children.

When the other funerals were held 'the full pathetic significance of a whole village in mourning was still more apparent'.

Again the village mills were silent and their occupants sorrowfully followed on the various routes of the dead for the different cottages. Spectators came from all areas around – the willingness to undertake a trip to these wild parts testifying to the dramatic interest that this village of mourning had aroused. The newspaper commented that:

> *'The sombre black of the crowd was only relieved by the fresh colour of the many beautiful wreaths.'*

As the cortege assembled, Mendelssohn's *O Rest in the Lord* was played followed by a simple service. As a tribute to the dead, Greenwood, the lay preacher, commented that someone had said to him: '… if this had been the funeral of a King there could not have been more respect shown'.

Other hymns included *Oh God our help in ages past* and the organist played the *Dead March* from Handel's *Saul*. Fellow workers carried the coffins of William and Alice Kershaw, whilst members of the Old Town Bowling Club carried Percy Roe's.

Later, the *Halifax Guardian*, who made an initial donation of one hundred shillings, opened a 'shilling fund' in aid of the orphans and dependent families. In Turner's case there were six children left. Though the eldest was married the youngest was only three. A local committee helped in the distribution of the funds and the lay preacher at Wainsgate Chapel – John Thomas Greenwood was soon authorised to make purchases for victims if needed urgently. He immediately arranged for some groceries from the Pecket Well Co-operative store for those who had no money to buy anything. Greenwood also started workshops at the chapel to raise funds.

When a Memorial service was held at Wainsgate Chapel, a church crowded with representatives from local organisations, mills and villagers were told by John Thomas Greenwood that the:

> *'gathering together of that great company was living proof that there was another victim associated with the calamity and that was Death itself'*.

Source:
Halifax Courier 1920

Part 3

Travel

12

Ferry Explosion

Hull

1837

'A frightful disaster took place on Wednesday last at Hull, from the bursting of the boiler of a steam-packet, by which a most melancholy loss of life was produced.'
Leeds Mercury, 10 June 1837

On Wednesday 7 June the early morning steam packet ferry *Union* was about to set off from Hull across the River Humber to Gainsborough in Lincolnshire. The bell rang for all passengers to go aboard before embarkation and there were almost 200 passengers on the deck, watching the crew prepare for departure, as well as the usual crowds on the dockside. It was a lovely morning and, for once, the river was calm and smooth so that everyone was looking forward to a pleasant voyage when an explosion ripped off the deck and forced out one side of the boat, which sank within a couple of minutes. The air was filled with smoke and steam. Human beings, their belongings, freight and bits of the ship were hurled high into the air, many being flung out into the depths of the river. Men with grappling irons reached out and dragged the mangled bodies to the side. Not only were those on board in danger. One poor man, Mr Matthews, was picked up by the force and thrown up onto the roof of Westerdale's block and tackle warehouse and some of the passengers of the *Don* packet boat from Thorne, moored nearby, were also injured when the iron crane from the *Union* fell. One of the *Don's* passengers, Rev Jackson, of the Methodist New Connexion, had only just arrived in Hull with his wife and six children on his way from Yarmouth to Doncaster to take up his new post. Initial reports suggested over a hundred had been killed but this proved wildly exaggerated. When the tide went down, bodies could be seen sticking out of the muddy banks and had to be recovered later.

Many of the bodies were taken to the police house in Blanket Row and an inquest to enquire into a number of the deaths was held there that same evening. Some had drowned as a result of being thrown into the river, whilst the others had sustained severe injuries in the explosion.

Israel Myers, a witness and survivor, stated that he was Jewish and a jeweller living in Nile Street, Hull. He had been on his way to Gainsborough, boarding the Union at around half past five in the morning and making his way to the 'after-end' of the ship, thus escaping injury but managed to get into a boat nearby as the *Union* sank. He remembered hearing a crackling noise, like sticks breaking but nothing unusual after that. He could see little because of the steam and smoke but helped rescue another young woman from the river and noted that the *Don*, which was nearby, was taking on many other passengers. He did however notice that someone, he thought the captain, went to the boiler and 'did something' at what he thought was the safety valve. A weight dropped off and after that the steam made more noise – 'it went off with greater violence than before'.

George Baines, an innkeeper from South Clifton, Nottinghamshire was scalded in the blast, some of the hot water affecting his eyes so was able to describe little of the aftermath of the explosion. His son, John, who was described as an apprentice to John Cottam, a grocer in East Retford, had been standing next to the boiler chimney shortly before the explosion. He heard the stewardess call out and three of the crew run towards the engine room. John sensibly moved away to where his father was standing and so he too escaped any real injury.

A further inquest was held at the infirmary. Two of the victims had originally been rescued alive but sixteen-year-old James Goddard died the morning after the explosion and Thomas Jacques had died at his home in Junction Street.

Police Constable number 64, William Abbott, said that he had been on East Pier that morning

Coroner:
J Thorney

Jury:
William Laverack, foreman
John Crosby Brown
Wiliam Jack
Thomas Peck
John Sutton Shopham
John Walkington
James Saner
Thomas Bethel Morley
Thomas MacTurk
Samuel Desforges
John Abraham
John King
Joseph Viccars
Charles Wray
William Couldrey

Jury:
From Payne Street:
Thomas Dykes, foreman
W N Depledge
From Wright Street:
John Bowes
John Collinson
From Storey Street:
Christopher Briggs
J B Fea
From Chariot Street:
George Cook
James Dawson
John Dobson
John Dobbs
Thomas Gibson
Benjamin Lumb
Marmaduke Baker
David Bensell?
William Jackson *of Albion Street*
John Black *of Beverley Road*

Sketch of the explosion, courtesy of Richard Hayton

and a man named Thompson, from Louth, had commented that there was something wrong with the ferry. They heard a loud bang as if something had fallen off and a few minutes later the boat blew up. Steam and smoke had been coming from the boiler on the side of the vessel, near the pier. He did not notice any steam coming from the safety valve or the chimney until the few seconds just before the explosion. Although hit on the head by wood from the exploding boat, he ran to the station house to give the alarm before returning to help.

This inquest was adjourned and resumed the following day. This time it was the turn of Abraham Townley Cudworth, the police inspector, who had heard the report of the explosion and organised the initial rescues, sending the injured to the Infirmary and the bodies of those killed to the station house. He described some of the injuries of the people – legs blown off, heads crushed and severe bruises and scalds. He attributed them all to the explosion. Charles Christopher Stephenson, a police inspector, had also been present, describing how he found other bodies and injured, though many of those recovered later seem to have been drowned or scalded to death. All the bodies were taken to the station house, where the jury inspected them.

Police Constable number 42, William Drake, had been on duty. He was left to guard the mass of goods and belongings which were picked up and put into the Victoria Rooms, later to be reclaimed by those who survived, or by the families of those who died.

At this point the jury all had to go to the house of William Lewis at

Wellington Street. He was part owner of the vessel and injured in the blast. He had gone on board, making his way eventually to the engine room. There was only a boy there, but Lewis saw that all four fire doors were open. He then tried the 'gage', which measures the height of the water in the boiler. The first emitted steam but the second let out water and he was unable to turn it off. Joseph Gamble, the engineer, then came in and he managed to turn the gage off. Lewis admitted that he often tried the gages of steam packets, which were considered safe if there was water in the bottom gage and steam in the top two. He stated that he had ordered some planks to be fitted to ensure the boiler remained in its proper place, even if the vessel was rolling.

Later evidence was heard from Thomas Longman, boilermaker and William Mail, a joiner, who had made four planks, fitted on the boiler to prevent the water flowing too fast. On examination, these were seen not to be charred, as would have been expected if the flue had been overheated. William Watson, who had previously worked on the *Union*, stated that the boat needed an unusual amount of water in order to get up steam for a vessel of her size, but he had explained this to his successor – Joseph Gamble.

Mr Lewis also stated that Matthew Gummerson, engineer of the *Vivid*, had recommended the engineer to him and also Mr Watson manager of Messrs Brownlow and Pearson, engine manufacturers, who both gave him a good reference. Gamble had completed a proper apprenticeship and was paid good wages – £2 14 shillings out of which he paid 8 shillings for his boy helper. The company paid for a second helper.

Captain Waterland, the master of the *Union*, was not quite so high in his recommendation of Gamble. Although he admitted that on that morning his own inspection of the boiler had not revealed anything wrong, he said that he

Humber Dock, Hull

'had occasion to find fault with the present engineer three or four times for putting too much weight on the safety-valve'.

James Overton, an engine and boilermaker from Hull, gave his 'expert witness' opinion on the boiler, which he said was in good condition when he had inspected it two months previously. The boiler had not been in use for the past six months, as the previous owners had sold it because it did not generate sufficient steam. He confirmed that the boiler was of good make, with high quality plates. In his opinion, the boiler would not have burst from pressure of the steam, but from an insufficient supply of water. This opinion was also shared by John Barrett and his son, Arthur Youle Barrett, boilermakers; John Malam, Joseph Vernon of Dock Street and Richard Holme.

However, Thomas John Pearson, a professor of chemistry at the Medical School, had examined various parts of the Union's boilers, which were lying on the quay and had come to the conclusion that the explosion was entirely due to steam pressure. William Walker of Lowgate and Dr Charles Wallich were of the same opinion. Yet Titus Rowbottom, a 'practical engineer' of Francis Street, gave further evidence. In his experience such explosions had always been as a result of the safety valve being fastened down or 'over weighted' or not running freely. If this were coupled with there being insufficient water then 'the explosion would take place sooner and with much more violence'.

The jury retired to consider their verdict which they finally agreed was:

'Whatever the immediate cause of the bursting of the boiler of the Union may have been, and on which there is much conflicting testimony, there is sufficient in the evidence to satisfy our minds that we are correct in returning a verdict of manslaughter against the engineer, Joseph Gamble.'

However, at his subsequent trial in York, he was discharged, the verdict there being that of 'accident'.

Those killed, or who died later in the infirmary, include:
Buried in Holy Trinity, Hull:

Luke Green, of Westwoodside, Lincolnshire.

James Goddard, engine boy of *Union*.

Mrs Rebecca Clegg, of Manchester, who was drowned whilst in her cabin.

Richmond Tomlinson, landlord of the *General Elliott*, High Street, Hull.

Rebecca Ferrier (or Farrier), of Mytongate, Hull, an old lady who earned a
living selling fruit and nuts to the passengers as they boarded the ferries.

John Weston, of Macclesfield.

Buried in Sculcoates, All Saints:
Alfred Pape, a traveller for Messrs Wharton and Hustwick, grocers, at

Junction Street, Hull.
Hannah Moody, New George Street.
Thomas Jacques, fancy chair maker, of Junction Street, Hull.

Buried at St Peter's, Drypool:
Robert Chatterton, brewer, of Hull.
Joseph Matthews, the Hull Dock Company's toll collector.
John Lowther, bricklayer, of Hull.

Buried in Lincolnshire:
Alice Dinsdale, a public house and shopkeeper.

Burial place unknown:
John Stephenson, a draper and grocer, from Haxey in Lincolnshire.
William and Arthur Hutchinson, sons of Mr Hutchinson, a builder in George Yard, Hull.
William Bland, engine boy of the *Union*.

Others were lucky and escaped with injuries:
Mr and Mrs Tonge, provision merchant, of Scale Lane (though their baby died).
Mr Hodkinson of East Retford.
George Baines and his son, of South Clifton, Nottinghamshire.
Mr Israel Myers of Hull.
Miss Snell of Addingfleet.
Mr and Miss Stewart of Storey Street, Hull.
Mrs Sampson, stewardess of the *Union*.
Mr William Lewis of Wellington Street, Hull, part owner of the *Union*.
Captain Waterland, master of the *Union* packet.
Mr Bass, steward of the *Union* was severely injured.
Joseph Gamble, the engineer.
Herr von Symmious or Symmous 'who had been giving lessons in the town on the use of the rifle' (*Leeds Mercury* 10 June 1837*).

Sources:
Leeds Mercury 1837
The Hull Advertiser 1837
Hull Post: The Journal for Humberside and the East Riding, No 7 1993
Recollections of Hull, Rev James Sibree
http://www.diplomate.freeserve.co.uk/whitton.htm

13

Lifeboat Disaster

Whitby

1861

There have been lifeboats at Whitby since 1802 when the first one arrived, being updated and supplemented later by two lifeboats, one kept to the west of the town, one to the east. On Friday evening, 8 February 1861 a north-easterly gale lashed itself into an 'intense fury' hitting the northern coastline in the early hours of Saturday morning. At Sandsend, just up the coast from Whitby, the crew of five from the Sunderland-based ship *Big John & Ann* were saved by a coble manned by fishermen John Storr, Robert Leadley, George Martin, William Tyerman, John Dixon, Henry Freeman and William Dryden. But these were not ordinary fishermen – they were also part of the voluntary crew of the Whitby lifeboat – a lifeboat that was to be launched five times in one day.

At 10am the lifeboat went to the rescue of the schooner *Gemma* that was sailing from Newcastle to London with a crew of four. All were saved. An hour and a half later the Prussian barque *Clara*, which had been built in Sunderland, ran aground near the *Gemma*. All the crew, from Memel, on the Baltic coast, were rescued before the ship broke up. Later a brig named *Utility* and a schooner named *Roe* ran aground almost together and again the lifeboat was launched, both times successfully taking the crews to safety.

The storm was still lashing the coast at mid-afternoon and ships such as the schooner *Flora* were heading for the safety of the harbour. Sailing just behind the *Flora* was the ship *Merchant*, but within sight of the harbour mouth, the *Merchant's* sails gave way and she was beached just north of the pier. Despite their exhaustion the lifeboat crew launched their little craft yet again to go to the rescue. Within 60 yards of the harbour mouth they were hit broadside by a huge wave that turned the boat right over, throwing all the crew into the sea. John Storr, who had been awarded a silver medal eight years previously to honour his work in the lifeboat, managed to clamber out onto the boat and others had lifebelts. Lifebuoys were thrown in to them from

Whitby harbour

the crowds on the harbour wall, many of whom were the wives and children of the crew who watched helplessly as the men drowned, only Henry Freeman being saved. For a while hopes were raised that William Tyerman and Isaac Dobson might have survived as they had managed to get under the boat and it was hoped that there was a pocket of air that could have saved them but this proved to be false hope and they also died. A lifeline was eventually thrown by mortar across to the ship *Merchant* and all five crew were hauled to safety.

Despite this disaster, when at 8pm the brig *Tribune* was beached, the old lifeboat was hauled from its mooring at Tatehill pier, launched into the harbour and rowed across before being lifted by crane and taken down to the beach. Further volunteers had come forward and they successfully reached the *Tribune*. Once told that all were out, the lifeboat returned safely to shore. It was only later that it was discovered that James Allan, of Cowes, had been left behind because he was already unconscious.

The bodies of the lifeboat crew were gradually recovered over the next few days as they were washed up onto the beach. They were considered such heroes that, not only was a local benevolent fund opened, but *The Times* newspaper in London also opened its own fund, which was simply known as the Times Fund. Benefits were paid to the widows, children and other dependents of the crew, though few of these are listed in the accounts. Specific mention is made of 'William Storr's sister who received two shillings and his child who, together with Matthew Leadley's child, received three

Whitby Lifeboat Museum display

shillings per week since they had lost both parents.' Other children received only two shillings each. Tickets were issued for flour, groceries, coal and 'Christmas festivities' for the children.

One-off payments were made to Thomas Robinson for trying to save the crew and the only surviving member of the crew, Henry Freeman, received £25. It had been his first venture with the lifeboats and he went on to serve as a crewmember for a further forty years. It was after this incident that the lifeboats were systematically replaced by more modern ones which did not 'turn turtle' in the waves.

The fund accounts give some idea of the later life of the crew's families. Ann Storr received a guinea for her 'motherly attention to her nephew, Ralph Storr'. The boy's mother, Jane, and his younger siblings, Barbara and John, had all died some time previously so Ralph was left an orphan when his father, William, died in the disaster.

Ralph himself did not receive any payments since he was seventeen by this time, but was obviously considered to be in need of a family home.

Rebecca Tyerman eventually became pregnant and the accounts record:

'Inasmuch as Rebecca Tyerman is now enceinte the sum of £20 be paid to her on her marriage provided she be married before the birth of the child'.

The marriage certificate details are copied into the accounts, showing that she married Henry Smith, a twenty-nine-year-old miner from Haggersgate, whose father is given as John, a wheelwright. Rebecca's age is given as twenty-seven and her father is William Andrew, a jet maker. How happy this marriage was is debatable. In 1868 an entry appears giving £1 to the 'husband of Rebecca Smith for kindness to his wife's children and encouragement of future behaviour'.

The recipients were expected to behave themselves. Esther Harland, widow of Robert, was struck off the list in 1870 for 'gross conduct' though she was later readmitted, probably to ensure that their daughter, Mary, was properly cared for. Jane Dobson does not seem to have been so lucky. She was struck off in 1865 for having an illegitimate child. Though the accounts record the death of the child, Jane does not seem to have earned readmittance to the funds.

In October 1864 Hannah Walker, widow of William, died leaving their daughter Alice an orphan at just fifteen. Her allowance was increased to 4s per week and she was sent to an industrial school where she could learn a trade to support herself.

Although there is a memorial plaque in St Mary's church, Whitby and the Whitby Lifeboat Museum includes the story in its exhibits, there are few original documents available. The Royal National Lifeboat Institute did not take over the Whitby lifeboat until after this disaster but most of the newspapers of the time included the story and they remain the best source of information.

As well as the Captain, John Storr, the crew who died included:
Robert Storr
Robert Harland
John Dixon
William Tyerman
John Philpot
Matthew Leadley
William Storr
William Walker
Isaac Dobson
Christopher Collins
George Martin
Robert Leadley

Left: Memorial to the lifeboat men, St Mary's Church, Whitby
Above: Memorial detail
Below: Gravestone of John Storr, St Mary's Church, Whitby

Committee of the Benevolent Fund:
Gideon Smales, Henry Simpson (of Bagdales), Henry Simpson (of Meadow Field), Thomas Moorwood (or Moulwood), Thomas Turnbull, William Steward, George Barwick, Isaac Peacock, Christopher Harrison, William Broderick, Edward William Chapman, Henry Robinson, John Stevenson, Francis Kildale Robinson and George Willis.

Sources:
North Yorkshire Archives, Northallerton
RNLI, Whitby Lifeboat Museum, Pier Road, Whitby YO21 3PU Tel: 01947 602001
www.whitby-yorkshire.co.uk/lifeboat/lifeboats.htm

14

Tram Accident

Huddersfield

1883

Huddersfield was the first town corporation to have its own municipally operated tram system, which opened in January 1883, and quickly established routes throughout the Corporation district. One of the most used routes was that running from the town centre out to Lindley, picking up and setting down workers at the mills along the way and taking visitors to the hospital, returning then to town down Trinity Street, West Parade and Westgate before turning sharply into Railway Street to St George's Square.

On Wednesday 4 July 1883 the tram set off from the *Fleece Inn*, Lindley on

Corner of Westgate, Huddersfield

its regular route back into town. It was a busy day and the tram was packed with passengers, to the extent that when Edwin Dyson of Westfield tried to get on, he had to run at great speed down the hill just to jump onto the step. He could get no further and soon decided to jump off again. It was a wise decision.

The tram careered on down Westgate, hurtling towards *Crown Hotel* corner. Dyson was not the only person to jump off; Joseph Wilson, of Lindley and Charles Sykes, of Marsh, jumped too as the vehicle swung around the corner. Screams could be heard such as: 'Put the brake on!' and others shouting: 'Look out the tram is coming down!' as it jolted along the rails for a few yards before finally toppling over. Passengers were flung together inside, whilst those riding on the open top were flung off onto the pavement below. Passers-by immediately rushed to help, though the crowd was also a hindrance, including one who was 'a respectably dressed elderly man who became quite angry when requested not to press forward'. Others were more helpful, lifting the injured from the roadway to the side and taking some into the *Temperance Hotel* and the estate buildings nearby until they could be removed to hospital. Dr Erson, of Lindley, was on board the tram itself and

Portland House, Lindley

was able to give invaluable assistance to the injured but it was not long before other doctors arrived and all the injured were taken to the hospital.

The tramcar was hauled back onto the lines as soon as it could be and taken to the tram shed, which was then in Northumberland Street. Back in Railway Street police officers had to be stationed to prevent the crowds blocking the street as everyone wanted to see the tram lines where the car had fallen. Opinions seemed to vary as to whether the car left the lines or not. Mr D M Sykes, of Longwood, stated that he was at the Cherry Tree Corner and that the car never left the metals until it fell over on its side nearly opposite the entrances of the estate buildings, yet the marks of the wheels where they left the line and up to the point where the car went completely over – a distance of about 24 paces – were clearly visible.

Immediately, the newspapers were full of letters and comments including suggestions for improving safety such as having toothed rails, appliances for gripping the rails or for 'dragging with great friction on the stones between the rails'. It was even suggested that the rails on the curve could be at different heights. The *Leeds Mercury* said that it was obvious that 'sufficient precautions have not yet been taken to ensure application of sufficient brake

Baptist church, Salendine Nook

power to the engines and cars'. One solution suggested was to bring the carriages as low down to the ground as possible, making them double the length with a connection similar to that of an engine and tender on railways and no top loading, which sounds similar to modern tram systems such as that in Sheffield.

Many of the injured had lucky escapes: the two daughters of Mrs Hanson, of Holly Bank Road, Annie, twelve and Harriet, fourteen, were riding on the outside of the tramcar, on the opposite side to that on which the car fell. They were thrown right over to near Messrs Sterry's shop and were picked up unconscious but later taken home. Mrs Peckett of Lindley, who was travelling with her little daughter, Helena, had her face badly cut from the car windows that were broken.

Others were not so lucky. Rowland Hall, a well-known retired manufacturer of Portland House in Lindley, was thrown from the top of the tramcar against a lamp post and seriously injured. He was transferred to the infirmary where his son-in-law, Charles Richard Garner of Reinwood Road, a monumental sculptor, visited him but Hall later died from the injuries received. He was buried in the graveyard of the Baptist church, Salendine Nook.

An initial inquest of identification was held before the serious business of finding out what happened began. This was not without controversy. General Hutchinson from the Board of Trade arrived and so the inquest was immediately moved to the Town Hall in order to discuss with the General whether the inquest should go ahead. It was finally agreed that it should, but the General would hold his own, independent inquiry and make his own report.

The jury also had a bone to pick with the Corporation. The jury felt that the engine should stay out of commission until after the enquiry, whilst the Corporation wanted it back in work as soon as possible. Not all the jury had been to see the engine, though it was pointed out that even if they did, they wouldn't understand it anyway! This prompted Mr Crowther, from the jury, to ask that, since General Hutchinson was not an engineer 'who was he going to depend on to explain when looking at the engine?'

The coroner replied that jurymen could not ask a question like that 'it was an extraordinary question to ask'. General Hutchinson represented a Government department and would make his own independent course in the matter. Hutchinson's inquiry would be very different to the coroner's inquest – his would be a 'more scientific or mechanical inquiry'. They all then went to view the engine.

Once there, it was Mr Wilkinson, of Messrs Wilkinson & Sons of Wigan, makers of the engine, who had to explain its workings to the jury and to General Hutchinson. The brakes were tested and seemed to be in perfect working order:

'and to fit the wheels so closely that when they were locked, a shaving put between the brake and the wheel could not be withdrawn'.

The engine was brought up to steam and run on the rails, but it was obvious something was wrong 'the engine rocked and snorted'.

Wilkinson suggested that it was unlikely to have been in that state before the accident and thought it was possible that it had been tampered with. This was altogether denied by the Tramways' superintendent and Councillor Armitage Haigh, Chairman of the Tramways Committee.

It became obvious that a further examination was needed. A police guard was set on the engine and it was agreed to test it again on Tuesday when Mr Middleton Pratt, an engineer from Huddersfield, could examine it and report back.

On Wednesday 11 July the report from the engineer was given privately to the Corporation but was not made public at that time.

The following day the inquest resumed, though again there was an argument as to whether the witnesses should be allowed to stay in the room whilst others were giving evidence, as the solicitors wanted, or whether they should stay outside, as the jury wanted. Eventually the solicitors won the day and the witnesses remained.

Margaret Miller, of Glen View, Edgerton, told the court that she had been on the tram, but got off at Greenhead Road. The conductor was on the top, collecting fares. She said the car was going faster than usual.

Alfred Crosland was next. He admitted touching the brake, but insisted he did it to avoid a calamity: 'I know what I am doing,' he said. He felt that the speed was too fast, and jumped off the tram. He said the brake 'felt different, tighter' after he had touched it. On being questioned further he said he couldn't tell whether it was on or off beforehand: 'I have never touched a brake before, I think I should have noticed if the brake was on'

General Hutchinson stated that it was impossible to turn it the wrong way, there was a catch to prevent it. The brake was turned to the right to put it on. Mr Crosland then stated: 'I turned it to the right, twice.' When asked if it 'ran back,' he admitted that he didn't know as he had 'held it'. A juryman commented that he didn't hold it after he had jumped off but this comment seems to have been ignored.

William Herbert Sykes, of

Jury:
W Radcliffe, St John's Road, foreman
Eli Whitwam, Alfred Sreet
Battye Royston, East Parade
John Crowther, Greenhead Road
Fred Eastwood, New North Road
Thornton Cliff, Colne Road
David Brown, Chapel Street
George William Crosland, New North Road
Allen Jackson, John William Street
B Jowett, West Parade
George Moxon, Trinity Street
Charles Riley, Henry Street
James Drake, New North Road

Lindley, got on the tram opposite the *Fleece Inn*. He sat near the engine and saw Fred Moore on the right hand side of the engine sitting with his wife, who had their baby on her knee. Rowland Hall was standing on the left hand side, leaning against the rails along with three others because there was no sitting room. The engine had been seven minutes late in setting off and began to go fast just above the *Old Hat Inn*. Just below the *Crown Inn* women began screaming, but as the tram was full right onto the steps there was no chance of getting off.

John Henry Sterry, tailor and outfitter, outside whose shop the tram had finally overbalanced, said that he often saw the car, generally travelling at about 8 miles per hour. Before the accident, it looked to be going at about 16 miles per hour.

John Rowe, of Hebble Terrace, Bradford Road, retired, was in Railway Street and saw the accident. There appeared to be many passengers, the heaviest load he'd seen.

Annie Crosland, who lived in West Parade, heard the engine from her house. It made a strange noise and then there was a large crack about 6 yards below her house and the engine began to go faster.

Joseph Theophilus Green, stationmaster, had seen the car on the curve and it looked to be going at 11 miles per hour. As he had considerable experience of engine speeds this was generally accepted as fairly accurate. He also said that he knew the sound of various vehicles and in his opinion, the brakes on the car

Fleece Inn, Lindley

and engine were off.

Alfred Crosland was then recalled to clarify his statement – he thought that after turning the brake there had been no effect on the speed, not that the speed had increased as his first statement had implied.

The Borough Surveyor, Richard Swarbrick Dugdale, said he had found a marked groove in the rails where the tram left the rails and stated that:

'if the wheels were revolving at the time the car came round the curve I should not have expected to find such a groove in the two sets as I did find,'

giving his opinion that the brakes were on at the time of the crash. He also suggested that the curve in the track was not that of the authorised plan. There had been a deviation of the outer curve, presumably to facilitate higher speeds. He agreed that a speed of 12 miles per hour was not safe in town.

Thomas Frederick Laxton stated that he had looked at the valves on the engine and found them closed, confirming that the brakes would not act if the valves were shut. Roscoe, the driver, had said he shut the valve against the steam that worked the automatic brakes. When asked if the driver could touch the screw handle and wheel so as to put the steam off, he replied: 'Yes, if he's fool big enough,' and went on to confirm that the driver was not supposed to touch the valves at all. Closing or opening them was under the control of the driver, but all engines had now been fitted a lock and chain on to prevent the valves being shut (he later admitted, to general laughter, that this would have no effect as the driver could easily get round it, but it was done to make the passengers feel safer!).

By 23 July Middleton Pratt submitted his report, supported by Joseph Hepworth, a fitter in his employ. He had found that the slide valve on the right hand side had moved on its spindle. The right hand piston was found to be smashed to bits and the piston rod bent. He was:

'of the opinion that the automatic brake was shut off (or inoperable for some other cause) the driver relying on reversing his engine and car brakes to control the load. The piston having smashed or the slide valve deranged or both, when the driver found the speed too high and reversed the engine it would be unable to answer him as one cylinder was quite useless and the other not sufficient to control the engine by itself.'

After some deliberation the jury's verdict was:
1 That the deceased died from the falling over of the tram car when running at excessive speed consequent upon the driver having lost control of his engine, through the breaking of one of the pistons thereby preventing him from effectively applying the reversing motion.

2 They severely censured the driver for having, in disobedience to orders, closed one entirely and the other partially, of the valves admitting the steam to the automatic brake thereby preventing any chance it might otherwise have had in coming into action.

The coroner wished to clarify this further:
'Accidental death with censure of the driver?' he queried.
'And the maker of the defective parts of the engine,' the jury replied.
'Not manslaughter?'
'Not manslaughter,' they confirmed.

They did, however, go on to endorse the specific recommendation made by Middleton Pratt, that an independent hand screw brake should be fitted on each engine with adaptation of a more effective means to prevent tampering with the automatic brake. They also suggested that the terminus of the Lindley and Edgerton tram on a double line of rails in Temple Street to avoid their converging at a sharp angle, and approved of the increased caution and decreased speed of the existing tram service. This, they said, should continue in a town like Huddersfield where 'gradients are severe, the curves sharp and the streets in many places narrow and often crowded'.

There was no joint funeral procession for the victims of the crash, each being buried in private ceremonies by their families in local churchyards.

Those who died:
Sarah Clegg, 42 Lindley
Rowland Hall, 60, manufacturer,
Portland House, Lindley
Joseph Halstead, mason, Birchencliffe
Annie Moore, 5 months
Fred Moore, 28, cotton spinner, Lindley
Mary Shaw, 52, wife of Jonathan Shaw,
Lindley
David Bertenshaw Taylor, 45,
rug maker, Outlane
Isabella Woodhouse, 66, Lindley

Those who were injured:
Jane H Barlow, Birkby
Emma Beaumont, Lindley
George Beaumont, Lindley
Alice Brook, Lindley
Polly Crowe, Oakes

William Henry Dean
Mrs Drayton, Bay Horse Inn, Lindley
Mrs Emmanuel Dyson, Lindley Moor
Mrs Joe Dyson
Wright Firth, Lindley
Annie Hanson, Lindley
Harriet Hanson, Lindley
Betsy Ann Hepworth, Lindley
Emily Liversedge, Milnsbridge
Richard Marsden, Ellend Edge
Mary Ann (Polly) Moore
James Roberts, Barkisland
Mrs Thomas Shaw, Marsh
John Shaw, Barkisland
Amos Sykes, Lindley
Joseph Wimpenny, Lindley
Mrs Lister Kaye, Lindley
Mrs Frederick Peckett, Oakes
Helena Peckett, Oakes

Source:
Huddersfield Daily Examiner 1883

15

Bullhouse Bridge Train Accident

Penistone

1884

On Wednesday afternoon, 16 July 1884, the 12.30pm train belonging to the Manchester, Sheffield and Lincolnshire Railway Company left Manchester station on its way to Sheffield. The driver, Samuel Cawood and his stoker, John Horne, had done the run many times in their years with the railway company and were looking forward to an uncomplicated journey. Looking back down the line from the engine, Samuel could see the horse box, the brake van followed by three coaches – with first, second and third class compartments – another brake van and six coaches. The long line ended with a third brake van, in charge of Stephen Phillipson, one of the guards.

The train chugged its way over the moors and through the long stretch of the Woodhead tunnel before beginning its descent to Penistone station, reaching a speed of 50 miles an hour as it passed the signals near the Bullhouse colliery. All went well until, just 2 miles short of Penistone, as the train passed over Bullhouse Bridge, there was a sudden bang and the brakes jerked on all along the length of the train. The engine, horsebox and first carriage slithered along the tracks, over the bridge and juddered to a halt, derailed but miraculously staying upright. But at this point the track curves

Manchester, Sheffield & Lincolnshire Railway/Great Central Railway
four-wheeled Tricomposite Carriage

slightly to the left. The bend was sufficient to throw the following carriages awry, breaking the coupling-bar. Three of the carriages fell from the bridge, smashing on the tarmac road below, whilst the others skidded and tumbled forty feet down the embankment to the nearby fields. Only two of the carriages landed on their wheels and as many of the passengers as possible hastily scrambled out.

Children from the local school saw what was happening and ran out to see, closely followed by their teacher, Joseph Ensor, who quickly rounded up his scholars and marched them back to school and safety. Help though came from the local villagers and men from Bullhouse colliery who had seen what was happening. The carriages, which had fallen on the road, were smashed to pieces and almost all of the passengers died, but many other survivors were crying out for help. As carefully as possible the injured were removed, the two local doctors rushing to their assistance. Others were taken to Sheffield and Leeds or, if not seriously injured, were taken onwards to their original destination. Breakdown gangs soon arrived from Sheffield and Gorton, which speeded up the removal of the injured and within a couple of hours the special train was ready to take them to Manchester. Dr Arthur Wilson, who was originally from Manchester himself, not only treated the injured but went

Wentworth Arms Hotel, Penistone

with them to Manchester Infirmary. Finally, sixteen bodies were removed to the carriage house of the *Wentworth Arms Hotel* in Penistone to await identification. Later, three more bodies were recovered and two died on the way to Manchester, making a total of twenty-one dead.

Needless to say, many 'officials' from the railway company were quickly on the scene, including Mr Sacre, engineer; W Bradley, superintendent of the line; Mr Pollitt, accountant; A Ormerod, mineral manager; Mr Hamilton, district superintendent; Mr J Lee, assistant superintendent; Mr Edge of the secretary's office and inspectors Burgess, Hunt and Shand.

Charles Wilson, of Manchester, survived and described his experiences:

'I and another gentleman who was in the carriage with me were thrown from our seats. The carriage seemed to take a leap and immediately there was a terrible crash. For a moment I was stunned … we were falling over a bridge upon a road that goes under the railway at that point. The depth at that point is sixteen to eighteen feet and when our carriage reached the road it was smashed to pieces… I was jammed with my legs between the seat of the carriage and a cushion. My right thigh was broken and I could not move … the carriage that followed the one in which I was riding was hanging over the bridge and threatened to fall upon me… some of the unfortunate people in the overhanging carriage were thrown out and fell out upon the road near me. Amongst them were three ladies who suffered terrible agony, and I, fastened between the woodwork, could render no assistance…We lay there for some time before anyone came to our assistance. Indeed, how could they in that out of the way place?'

The Rev Venable Williams, of Colwyn Bay, was also on the train, travelling in a carriage that, he said, was full of Germans who were returning to Germany via Grimsby. When their carriage landed at the bottom of the embankment, they helped Rev Williams out of the carriage. He happened to be carrying a 'railway key' with which they were able to open the carriage door. Williams then went back down the line to the signal box to stop any further trains before returning to help at the scene of the wreck.

Thomas Morley, of Barnsley, was a wagon inspector and had been on the train on his way to Penistone. He too helped many of the passengers to climb out of the carriages. Mrs Dickinson, of South Kensington, had been travelling with a small child and its nurse. Both women were badly injured, though the child escaped with minor cuts and bruises. The nurse, Ann Lee (or Lea), was not

expected to survive.

Police Superintendent Wright, of Pitsmoor, Sheffield said he had been travelling on trains for thirty-six years and this was the first accident he had had.

A number of people were working in the fields round about and ran to help. James Wagstaff of Millhouse was working about half a mile away and had a clear view of the accident. He heard a 'fearful din' and saw the engine and horsebox steaming away from the carriages. He ran to assist and 'could distinctly hear the cries and groans' of the passengers. As he helped remove the injured, they were laid out on the cushions taken from the carriages.

At the inquest each body had to be identified by a friend or relative. William Gane, of Boston, Lincs, a certified teacher, stated that he had seen the dead bodies and recognised Mary Stower, forty-five, and the wife of Jacob Singleton Stower, a traveller for Wine and Spirit Merchants and Mary Ann Spencer, sixty-five, widow. She lived with Mary Stower in Boston, Lincolnshire.

Mary Dawson, of Royle, was only thirty-five and the daughter of James, a farmer. They appear to have been fairly well off since Reverend Ellerbeck of

Pennine railway line at Bullhouse Bridge, now part of the TransPennine Trail

Nottinghamshire whom she was going to visit described her as 'Proprietor of Land'.

Emma Mary Jones, seventeen, was the daughter of James Jones, engineer and ironfounder of Birkenhead, deceased. Her uncle, Thomas Turton, also an iron founder, had travelled with her across the river and seen her into a cab to take her to Central Station for her journey to Sheffield.

John Shorrock or Sharrock was an iron founder and loom maker, of Darwen, employing over 200 people. Both he and his wife, Harriet, were killed.

Mr John Proctor Woodhead, forty-one, valuer and insurance agent, of Manchester and Bridge House, Baguley. His younger brother, James, came to identify his body and said that he didn't even know John had been going away.

The Barwick family, consisting of Martha Barwick, mother of Edith, six, Archibald, two, and Beatrice, just five weeks old, were travelling to St Neots in Huntingdon together with Martha's sister, seventeen-year-old Agnes Clotilda Constance Ekins, a draper's assistant in Manchester. Her father, James Morton Ekins, had died some time previously so another relative, Alfred David Ekins, identified her. Martha, wife of Edward Barwick, a shirt manufacturer from Birmingham, had been born in Huntingdon and was probably going to visit relatives there. Agnes, and the three little children were all killed instantly. Martha, though badly injured, survived and was taken to Manchester Infirmary.

Rachel Coates or Coats, was a widow who lived with two of her daughters in Prescot, near Blackburn, Lancashire. Her son, Rev John M Coates, identified the body of his mother, who had been on her way to visit him in Moulton, Lincolnshire where he was curate. He had not seen her for some time and she was probably going to visit to see her new little grandchild, Alice, who was just three months old. When Rachel failed to arrive in Lincolnshire her son took a train to Manchester and enquired at the infirmary. Not finding her there he went to Penistone and found her amongst the dead. Ironically, his father had also been killed in a rail crash twenty-five years previously.

Albert James Gridlestone, twelve, outfitters assistant of Orwell Road, Liverpool was identified by his father, James, who had last seen him at half past seven the previous morning when he had asked his daughter Elizabeth to take the lad to Central Station to catch the train in order to visit his aunt in Newark.

Carrie (or Clarrie) Eddleston (or Edelstein) from York was the widow of George Richard Edelstein, a general merchant. She was originally reported dead, but on arrival at the infirmary was found to be clinging to life though severely injured. She finally died towards the end of August and was identified by John Malin Edelstein of Warrington, a file and pin manufacturer and her brother-in-law.

Agnes Gould was only seventeen. Her father having died previously, it was left to her brother, Thomas, to identify her.

James N Poole, originally from Bristol but had come up to Prestwich to work for J Wrigley & Sons, paper makers of Bury, where he was manager of their warehouse. He was taken to Manchester badly injured and he too died within a fortnight.

Other victims of the crash include:
Ann Tetlow, fifty, of independent means, Skirden House, Bolton by Bolland.
Mrs Martin, forty, Park Lane, Liverpool.
Annie Rawlings, forty-seven, wife of Frederick Rawlings, a herbalist of Reddish in Lancashire.
Annie Lee/Lea, nurse, Cheshire.
Michael Turner or Durkan, labourer, from Cork.
Robert Aldred Marshall, thirty-one, a mining engineer.
Mr Shackleton, of Sheffield.
Massey Bromley, engineer and locomotive Superintendent for GER of Victoria Street, Westminster.
Plus body of a girl dressed in a silk skirt and black jacket was found but not identified.

The scattered remains of the passengers' belongings were collected together and taken to Penistone. Some baggage escaped unscathed, including the forlorn pram belonging to the two little Barwick children who were killed, along with their elder sister and aunt.

Some mysteries arose from the accident. One man from Liverpool had seen his wife off earlier. A woman in the same carriage as his wife had died, yet he could not find his wife's body amongst the dead, nor was she in the infirmary. Miss Dawson, of Clitheroe, had definitely been in a carriage with Ann Tetlow who was killed. Rev Ellerbeck, who she had been going to visit, identified Miss Tetlow's body but he could find no trace of Miss Dawson.

The inquest opened on Thursday 17 July before Thomas Taylor, the district coroner. Mr Underdown, the general manager of the railway company, expressed the 'great grief' they all felt at this 'sad calamity'. The jury and other officials then went off by a special train to the scene of the accident but as there was no further evidence at that time, the inquest was adjourned. There was also to be an official government enquiry into the accident. Initially the driver and guard were questioned. Samuel Cawood the driver insisted he had examined the train before leaving Manchester and noted nothing amiss.

James Irving, guard on the train, described how the van came off the line, saying it:

'gave a bound or two and the next moment was on its side. It then shot along the bottom of the adjoining composite carriage ahead of it and which was upside down. The wheels of the carriage came through the sides of the van. We seemed to go a little way and then stop. On looking round I saw the whole of the train, excepting the engine, tender and horse box which were on the rails, down the side of the embankment, resting on the wall. The engine had gone perhaps 140 or 150 yards ahead; some of the carriages were upside down. I ran to the signal box and directed the man to signal all off from Hazelhead and other parts and wired for assistance from Penistone. I then went to the engine to get on to Penistone for help but found it was disabled and returned to the train. I assisted several persons to escape from the wreck and then hurried by road to Penistone. I returned from Penistone by the relief train about two o'clock and by that time the people in the neighbourhood had extricated passengers who were seriously hurt. The engine had run well for nine months. I never heard a flaw in it. It is difficult to tell what rate we came through the tunnel; perhaps 30 miles per hour or 40 down the incline. The brake was applied [Smith vacuum] and it acted.'

Henry Baxter, signalman at the box nearest the Bullhouse colliery, described his view of the event:

'The train seemed to pass my box at the ordinary speed and there was nothing unusual about it. When the engine passed the signal box I heard a heavy thud. Then I saw the carriages away to the left to the outside of the curve. The carriages in the centre of the train swayed, first running on one wheel until they got to the bridge. As soon as the engine and horse box passed the bridge the couplings broke and the carriages went over the embankment. They seemed to slide down. I at once placed all the signals at danger. I have never seen any carriages away on passing the place before.'

The main consideration was to consider what exactly had caused the accident and who was to blame. It was obvious that the axle had broken but no one could say why.

R McDermott, gave evidence on the condition of the crank, showing that it had a flaw in it about one inch long. The crank had only been used one sixth of the usual time and he felt it should have been safe to go round the bend at fifty mph. Charles Sacre, chief engineer of the Manchester, Sheffield and Lincolnshire Railway, considered the fracture a 'growing one', which no examination could have detected.

However, this was disputed by Joseph Pepper, the managing director of Messrs Taylor Bros, Leeds, manufacturers of iron and steel for railway and marine purposes, who had made the broken crank axle in 1883. He considered that the fracture was a 'good, clear fibrous fracture, quite free from any original flaw or defect whatsoever'. He went on to describe how he had cut a piece from behind the fracture and divided it into four pieces to test its tensile strength, and also taken the unbroken arm of the crank axle, placed it under a falling weight at Gorton and for six hours constant and ineffectual attempts were made to break it. The weight used was 16 hundredweight and fell from various heights.

The steel used was best quality and a man with thirty years experience had forged the crank. Pepper was sure there was no flaw giving his opinion that the outside rod had snapped first:

'that part of it attached to the outside crank at the end would suddenly fly round and being much longer than the radius of the wheel it would necessarily come into contact with the permanent way which would give a great shock to the inner crank axle. The rod itself was bent and on the inside corner of the end towards the engine was the mark of heavy blows. The crank arm was fractured in two places and the pillar of the axle box was bent and broken.'

John Atkinson, the forge man who had made the axle, said he had forged thousands of crank axles. He too could see no evidence of a growing flaw, but thought rather that the axle had 'gone all at once'.

The railway company employees felt completely differently. Stanhope Perkins, superintendent of Gorton Works, of Manchester, Sheffield and Lincolnshire Railway, had examined the axle and thought there was a flaw in it. It was a growing flaw. The rod breaking might throw a strain on the crank axle and break it but in his opinion in this case the crank axle went first.

Mr Sacre, engineer, had no doubt about the fact that there was a growing fracture. He had thirty-six years experience in these matters and seen many broken cranks. It was a 'bolt and socket' fracture that would not have been immediately apparent.

Two more engineers were asked about the axle. Again the opinion differed. John Hopkinson, consulting engineer of Wren & Hopkinson of Manchester, stated that in his opinion the accident was caused by the breaking of the crank web of the axle due to an internal strain in the web, produced when the steel was hot or in the process of forging or when cooling down. No brake could have affected the outcome – it was not relevant to the accident. However, Ernest Latham, mechanical engineer, Birkenhead, was of the opinion that 'for some time there had been a crack through the inner surface of the web and it ought to have been detected by examination'.

The coroner in summing up decided that there was no evidence of neglect by the company or its servants; the final verdict being death by misadventure.

The government inquiry agreed that cause of accident was the breaking of the outside web of the right hand crank on the driving axle, whilst the engine was running at a speed of something under 50 miles an hour. It could not have been foreseen or prevented.

However, he commented on the brakes. Although they had been activated when the coupling broke, the carriages had no mechanism to stop them and thus made the accident worse:

'If fitted with an automatic brake, which would have remained on when the carriages parted from the engine, the [speed of the] *first four or five carriages ... would have been reduced and there would have been little damage.'*

He also advised a more thorough inspection of the cranks.

His final comments referred to one passenger's evidence that he had had to instruct the signalman to set the signals at danger, saying pointedly that there was absolutely no evidence that this was the case.

In the midst of all this, the Manchester, Sheffield and Lincolnshire Railway had held its ordinary half-yearly meeting of shareholders. Sir Edward Watkin MP, chairman of the Board, expressed the feeling that:

'To everybody concerned this unfortunate accident had given the deepest pain and sorrow.'

However, he was quick to point out, despite the fact that the inquest had not at that point reached its final verdict, that:

'The Accident could not be foreseen or provided against therefore there was no pecuniary liability.'

which was probably a relief to the shareholders.

To give him his due, he had offered for himself, not for the Board, to provide help in cases of severe need.

He also gave thanks to the people on the spot: Mr Underdown, Mr Ross, Mr Sacre, Mr Bradley and others, also the shareholder Mr Hinchliffe of Bulhouse Colliery and 'his good wife' Mrs Judith Hinchliffe, their son and daughter-in-law, and the men who had given assistance.

Notes:

A Bogie is a structure underneath a train to which wheel axles are fastened.

A Brake van is coupled at the end of a freight train and is usually manned.

A continuous brake is a train brake that provides for control of the brake on every vehicle in the train and is automatic to emergency stop in the case of loss of control.

The crank axle is the strongest axle.

A crank is the shaped bend in an axle which changes the piston movement into rotational movement of the wheels.

Sources:

C493/K/2/1/3 Taylor notebooks – coroner's inquest

www.vintagecarriagestrust.org/Collection.htm

Huddersfield Daily Examiner 1884

16

———

Rail Disaster

Thirsk

1892

'*A tangled mass of shapeless ironwork that once was a railway engine, a torn and shattered framework that posed as a Pullman car but a few hours ago, three twisted rails and half burnt splinters of wood are all that remain to tell the passers-by as the trains again speed their way north and south, of the terrible calamity which has sent such a thrill through the whole of Great Britain.*'

On 2 November 1892 the Edinburgh to London express was finally ready to set off. It was so long it had been decided to split it into two sections and everyone was impatient to get going including the Marquis of Tweedale, the Marquis of Huntly, General Lambton and Mr Kynoch, a director of Highland Railway who were comfortably seated in the Pullman car.

The first section set off, followed a few minutes later by the second which consisted of a Newcastle engine of the four-wheel-coupled type; a van containing luggage only; a third-class carriage; the Pullman sleeping car; two ordinary East coast sleeping carriages; another luggage van; two composite carriages; a fish van; a horse box with three horses for London and the rear guard's van, where the guard, George Bean, kept an eye events while the conductor, Richard Wimpress, should have been found at the front of the train, but at Darlington he

APPALLING RAILWAY DISASTER.

———

THE "FLYING SCOTSMAN" IN COLLISION AT THIRSK.

———

DESTRUCTION OF THE TRAIN BY FIRE.

———

NINE PASSENGERS AND A GUARD KILLED.

———

HEARTRENDING SCENES.

———

Headline, Leeds Mercury

changed to the centre van to arrange some parcels and luggage for delivery at York. He owed his life to this simple change.

The train made good time coming down through Scotland and resumed its journey on time from Darlington. Meanwhile, at Northallerton, the first portion of the mail passed through and a goods train of thirty-five trucks, laden with pig-iron and general merchandise was then sent out of that station to Thirsk, where it should have left the line clear for the second section of the London train. For some reason, the train was stopped by the signals at Manor House, a signal cabin about 3 miles to the north of Thirsk junction and while the goods train was standing in the fog the second section of the mail was signalled from Otterington and, all signals being off, advanced at full speed, running straight into the goods train. The goods guard was killed on the spot.

The express train, having struck the goods van, shot round at right angles while the front van and the third class carriage attached to it were smashed to pieces. The two ordinary sleeping cars, the composite carriage and also the guards van ploughed over these two carriages, balancing precariously on top in a broken heap. The Pullman car, being made of better materials, was thrown off its wheels, skidded over the top of the wreckage, landing on the other side of the engine. The bodywork was much battered, but most of the windows remained unbroken and the occupants escaped with cuts and bruises.

Although the whole of the train was derailed, the last half was not badly damaged though all the lamps were extinguished.

Wimpress, the conductor and Bean, the guard, clambered out of the wreckage and relit their lamps. Bean immediately ran to the signal box to stop the trains then back to the 'down' line to ensure no trains came from that direction either. Telegrams were immediately sent from the Manor House cabin to Thirsk and from Thirsk to York, where a special train was sent out, with Dr Anderson, Dr Gosling, Mr Steel (assistant passenger superintendent) and Mr Harper the York Stationmaster taking a number of ambulance men with them. A breakdown gang followed as soon as possible.

Unfortunately, at the scene of the accident, things were getting worse. This was, of course, a steam train, derailed and covered with the remains of a number of carriages. Shortly after the collision the fire of the express engine set fire to the woodwork that was piled above and around it, and fed by the gas with which the train had been lighted the flames quickly spread, showing a red glow in the heart of the fog which surrounded the scene. The passengers who escaped injury themselves rushed to rescue others, a job which grew more and more hazardous as the fire spread. Though a railway fire engine was quickly brought from York by special train, when, late in the afternoon, the fire finally died down it was only because there was nothing left to burn. All that remained was an ugly heap of twisted iron and cinders.

As the bodies were carried from the wreckage they were taken to a nearby field and laid there for identification. Many of the injured were taken to the cottages nearby whilst others were removed to Thirsk Lambert Memorial Hospital. Most of the survivors continued their journey by special train to York and then onwards to their original destination.

One passenger gave a graphic description of the disaster. Mr R A Hodgson, of Bryanston Square, London, said:

'We reached Newcastle sometime before two in the morning. Everything seemed to be all right until there was a sudden crash and I saw the sides of the carriage caving in 'tent fashion'. I instantly realised the danger and exclaimed to two ladies who were in the third-class compartment in which I was: "For God's sake, put your legs on the seat." We had hardly done this before the seats crushed together. I crawled out through the window and lifted out the two ladies. I then assisted lifting out some of the other passengers, about fifteen more I should think and placed them at the side of the line. I gave what assistance I could in removing the dead and injured. Most of the passengers who were not seriously injured lost their heads and husbands and wives were crying piteously after their dear ones. I took upon myself the responsibility of getting out the luggage from the van near the engine. I

Thirsk Lambert Memorial Hospital

remember especially securing the Leeds and other mails. The driver of the express had been very badly injured and was covered with blood and dirt and was shockingly disfigured. I went to assist to carry him to the side of the line and he said: "Never mind me, go and help some of the other poor passengers". It was a brave thing to say, but we afterwards dragged him on a cushion to a safer place. One of the most shocking sights was that of a woman who had been thrown by the collision under the engine and was literally burned to death. We helped the husband out. He was injured and came to us crying: "My poor wife is under there." It was quite impossible for us to save her as the flames were blazing furiously. I never want to go through such an experience again.'

Among the survivors was a young married man named McKenzie, a tailors' cutter who was travelling to London with his wife, where they proposed to set up house. With them they carried their savings – a sum of £20. After the collision McKenzie found himself under a pile of debris. It was all darkness for a time, but then a light came. 'I looked for my wife and saw her lying with a beam across her chest and her hands held up. I spoke to her and she gave me no answer. Her name is among the list of the dead.'

Some were critical of the action taken by the railway staff. Rev J S Forsyth of the Caledonian Asylum, Caledonian Road, London, a minister of the Scotch Church, had been dozing in the corner of a carriage, also occupied by his friend, John Lumsden Stuart and a lady and her two children. The woman began shrieking and though he tried his best to calm her:

'Her fears were not allayed by the folly of an individual, who having liberated himself, went down the line shouting: "There's another train coming along, which of course was an alarm equally absurd and groundless."

It was very cold that morning and some passengers lit a fire for the survivors to huddle around:

'We suffered the greatest discomfort until the arrival of the relief train from Thirsk about two hours later with squad of about forty men, some of whom were railway employees but, ridiculously enough, they had brought with them no implements or ambulances, so that the work of extricating the dead and dying had to be performed by improvised appliances. I heard one poor child, who was burnt to death, shrieking for help but nothing could be done for it and the same occurred in the case of a young lady who unfortunately, poor creature, died amidst the terrible wreckage. Lord Tweedale, I may say, acted very kindly and did all in his power to assist others.'

This suggestion, that there was little medical relief brought, was later refuted. Dr Hartley, who attended, commented on the efficient work of the railway staff, many of whom had attended St John's Ambulance training courses:

'John S Sadler, a porter at Thirsk station, had already attended to Ewart's thigh before our arrival and undoubtedly prevented the fracture becoming a compound one …

The lies in the papers about this accident were simply extraordinary – everything was done for the sufferers that was possible and Mrs Coulson of Manor Farm and the cottagers wives were most attentive and kind.'

The *Leeds Mercury* newspaper made the comment that:

'It used to be said, with some great cynicism, that serious railway accidents would be events of frequent occurrences till the mangled remains of a railway director were taken from the wreck caused by the collision.'

But the Pullman carriage at the front of the train housed the Marquis of Tweedale, Chairman of the North British Railway Company, General Lambton, Mr Kynoch, director of Highland Railway and the Marquis of Huntly and though:

'That vehicle was tossed in the air and thrown violently forward a considerable distance, and yet, as if by a miracle, the occupants were comparatively unhurt.'

There was much speculation as to the cause of the crash as this was not a busy junction 'but at a solitary signal cabin at a comparatively quiet part of the system'. It was immediately decided that the incident might have been caused by a misjudgement of the signalman, who appeared to have given the signal 'line clear' forgetting the presence of the goods train – a mineral train from Middlesbrough. The express train therefore was running at 'express speed'. The newspaper asked whether it was 'only by this fearful accident and sacrifice of life that a grave defect in the working of the traffic on this part of the North Eastern main line has been discovered?'

The signalman, Holmes, was suspended from duty pending an inquiry.

On Thursday afternoon the inquest, under the aegis of Mr J S Walton, was opened in the general waiting room on the down platform at Thirsk Junction station. North Eastern Railway were represented by Kaye Butterworth, solicitor; John Welburn, general passenger superintendent; Mr C Steel, assistant superintendent, York; Mr J Dobie, police superintendent; Sir Charles Firth, president of the West Yorkshire Fire Brigade attended. E Harford, general secretary of Amalgamated Society of Railway Servants represented the suspended signalman, Holmes.

The jury viewed the bodies in the waiting room of the opposite platform. Evidence of identification was given as Inspector Cooke read a list of articles found in the possession of each body and later went to view the scene of the accident before the inquest was adjourned.

The signalman, James Holmes, explained the events of the 24 hours prior to the accident:

'I was on duty from six o'clock on Monday evening to six o'clock on Tuesday morning. I went on again at eight o'clock on Tuesday evening. I had a child died suddenly on Tuesday and had a lot of running about during the day. I applied to my superior officer at Otterington station for relief from duty on Tuesday night. This would be about half past two in the afternoon… he said he would see what he could do and I was to come up again about the usual time for going on duty, and he would be able to tell me what the reply was from York.

I told him the circumstances why I wanted relief saying I did not feel fit for duty. I went to South Otterington to wire for my mother to come and stay with my wife and at the same time told the police constable about the child's death and then returned to Thornton-le-moor. I had a lot of running about

Thirsk railway station

during the afternoon in connection with the death of the child. I went again to Otterington station to meet the 6.05pm train from Thirsk thinking my mother might come with it and also to see as to the reply from York as to relief. I asked Mr Kirby what the reply was and he said Mr Pick regretted to say he could not relieve me that night. I said: "It is a bad job, Mr Kirby I don't feel fit for it but I'll go and do the best I can." I waited a few minutes for the train and I got permission for my mate to stay on duty for me a while...

I was in bed from about 7.30am or 7.45am to 9am I then had a cup of tea which my wife brought me. I had the child in bed with me then. I should fall asleep again about 9.45am and sleep until 11.45am when my wife found the child in a fit...

I then went to Otterington station and got a goods train to Northallerton ... I went to the doctor's but found him out, and as I learned he might have been to Thornton-le-Moor I walked back and got home about 2pm... I went to Otterington village calling at the station and then back home. I did not feel well myself ... I finished about 5pm and was on the run almost all the time. I walked about sixteen miles during day – Manor House cabin is about two and a half miles from my dwelling house ...'

Henry Eden, signalman at Otterington station, was on duty when the accident happened and explained the timing of events:

3.37am	The first part of the express went through.
	He gave his reply 'line clear'.
3.47am	Sent 'be ready for goods train'.
3.58am	Received 'be ready for second part of express'.
4.01am	Second express passed.
4.02am	Message from Manor House asking if it was 'EP' express train

going through. Eden confirmed this. He also had to confess that he had written in the incorrect time at 3.47, entering this as 4.47 and later had to alter his book.

The other signalmen confirmed the general timings for when the express train passed their box.

Thomas Kirby, the South Otterington station master, was quickly informed of the disaster by Henry Eden and together they organised assistance. They arrived back at the scene around half past four and began the task of removing bodies from the wreckage. He confirmed sending a telegram to his superior that simply said:

'Can you send relief to Manor House cabin tonight Holmes child dead'

The reply, sent by the clerk on duty, not Thomas Pick, the inspector, was equally brief:

'Cannot relieve Holmes tonight.'

The jury immediately queried why Kirby had not been more specific that Holmes had said he 'felt unfit for duty'. Kirby replied that he had thought his message sufficient.

Thomas Pick, of York, a traffic inspector for North Eastern Railways, explained that he had been absent when the telegram arrived but his clerk Harland was authorised to make the decision though usually he asked before giving definite orders. On this particular night, Harland could not reach Pick who had been in Huttons Ambo. Pick then surprised the jury by informing them that, in fact, the cabin could simply have been closed – and Kirby had the authority to do so.

Joseph Barnes, from Middlesbrough, engine driver of the goods train, described his vehicle as having thirty-five wagons and a van. It was laden with metal, timber and iron. After waiting for five minutes at Manor House

York Crown Court

he said the home board [signal] fell and so he set off. As he passed the cabin, the signalman shouted out asking if the distant signal was on when he'd passed it and 'I answered that it was'. Half the train passed the cabin when the rear of it was run into by something. The driver went forward to the advance signal and then stopped. On looking back he found the express train had run into the rear of the goods train. Barnes confirmed that the night was foggy but insisted that he could see the signals at 30 yards and that the signalman 'could see my train'. His fireman, John William Fenna of Newport, confirmed these events but also added that 'the whistle had not sounded before starting'.

This point was taken up again when John Welburn, of York, Superintendent of the North Eastern Railways was questioned. He produced the rulebook, which stated:

'In case of detention at a home or starting signal, the engine driver must sound his whistle and if still detained the guard or fireman must go to the signal box and remind the signalman of the position of the train or engine and remain there until the signalman can give permission to go forward. In foggy weather or during falling snow, the guard or fireman must immediately upon the train or engine coming to a stand, proceed to the signal box.'

Whilst he couldn't say that sounding the whistle would have prevented the accident it would certainly have reminded Holmes of the presence of the goods train.

On 6 December the trial of Signalman James Holmes began before Justice Charles at York Assizes. Holmes was indicted for the manslaughter of the guard, George Petch, one of the victims of the rail crash.

Prosecution – Mr Waddy QC, MP and Mr Blake.

Defence – E Tindail Atkinson QC and Mr Charles Mellor.

Mr T Milvain QC and Mr Dent watched the proceedings on behalf of the North Eastern Railway Company.

The tale of the events was repeated, Kirby adding that after the accident, Holmes had admitted, 'it is all my fault, Mr Kirby. There is no-one else to blame but me.'

Kirby did not think the man was incapable or he would have closed the cabin. When asked: 'Could you have closed the cabin and prevented the accident?' he replied: 'Yes.'

The question of relief was looked at more closely. Thomas Pick, traffic inspector of the NERC, produced Holmes' entry book. He confirmed that whilst he was away a telegram had been received from Otterington:

'Can you send relief to Manor House Cabin tonight?'

His assistant sent the reply: 'No relief can be sent'. If relief had been available, it would have been sent. But there was an alternative: to close the cabin. 'Could he do that?'

'Yes, there is a rule that when the lamp goes out, the cabin can be closed, and this can be used at the discretion of those in charge.'

Holmes, apparently, was not told the signal cabin could also be closed in the case of illness, though Pick insisted that he'd 'never allow a man on duty unfit'.

There were 17 relief signalmen in York, 283 signalmen and 3 inspectors. But there had been floods and another accident because of the floods and all relief men were unavailable. The jury wanted to know what else could have been done:

'So if no-one was available, the alternative would be to close the station?'
'Yes.'
'Why was this not done?'
'I didn't know he was unfit.'
'Did the station master at Otterington have the power to close the cabin?'
'Yes.'

Henry Eden, signalman at Otterington station, was on duty when the accident happened and explained the timing of events:

> *He then received a message from Holmes asking if it was 'EP' (express passenger) and replied that it was. He thought this was odd for Holmes to be asking what train it was so stopped to watch from the window and heard the crash. Then Holmes sent message: 'Tell Mr Kirby express run into goods train'. He'd seen Holmes at a quarter to eight that evening and he was 'done up to start with'. Holmes had said: 'Really, Harry, I haven't been off my legs since twelve o'clock'.*

Joseph Barnes, engine driver of the goods train: 'When I arrived at Manor House Cabin the signals were at danger and he applied the brakes and stopped. They stood for four or five minutes when the signals went down and they proceeded. I stopped again at the advance and the collision happened almost immediately.' He found the guard was killed.

There were no witnesses for the defence.

Mr Atkinson admitted negligence and asked the jury to consider the man's condition through his child's death and his wife's illness.

The jury verdict was guilty, with a recommendation to mercy.

The judge agreed with their verdict and the recommendation to mercy. Holmes was bound over for £50 'in his own recognisance' to come to court for judgement. At the decision there was loud cheering, the prisoner crying bitterly. His wife in the public gallery fainted.

Some magazines had been running advertisements for personal insurance and, surprisingly, many paid out the compensation provided the details had been completed, even though the papers were not signed.

List of killed:

John H Lew, potato salesman, Spitalfields Market, London (had in his possession current number of *Tit Bits*, with insurance), buried in Abney Cemetery, London. He had also been a churchwarden at Spitalfields.

James J Anderson, Panmure Street, Dundee (had in his possession insurances amounting to £2,750. These were *Tit Bits* for £100, *Answers* for £1000, and *Great Thoughts* for £1000, *Christian Herald* £500 and also *Person's Weekly* insurance for accidents from football).

Mr J Boswell Hill, George Street, Edinburgh (had in his possession railway insurance ticket for £200), interred at Dean Cemetery, Edinburgh.

Captain Duncan McLeod, 42nd Highlanders (Black Watch), interred at Stirling.

George Petch, guard of the goods train, who had been living at

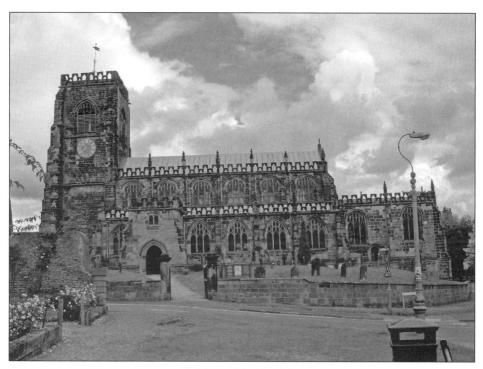

St Mary's Church, Thirsk

Middlesbrough with his wife and seven children, was interred at Middlesbrough New Cemetery, Alexandria, Dunbartonshire.

Miss Ann Glen McCullock, Gillmore Street, Alexandria, Dumbartonshire, and her niece, Charlotte Hamilton. Both were buried in the parish church, Thirsk

Mr R M (J H) Boyle, traveller in the service of Augenor & Co, music publishers, 85 Newgate St, London.

Mrs McKenzie, Leven Place (Street), Edinburgh.

Mr Hugh P Brodie, Plym (Railway) Villa, Walwood Road, Leytonstone, London (had in his possession an insurance ticket for £200).

Injured:

Lady Stuart, Harrington Gardens, London.

David McCullock, brother of the above named Miss McCulloch and uncle of the little girl, Lottie Hamilton.

Alexander McKenzie, Leven Road, Edinburgh, husband of Mrs McKenzie, one of the killed.

Rose White, Bickley, near London (of the Boosey Theatrical Company).

Sarah Robinson, Monstrose.

Provost Sutherland, Bathgate.

R A Hodgson, Upper George Street, Bryarston Sq, London.

Mrs Fansell? Chatsworth Square, London.

Mrs Dad(d), Glentarra, Aberdeen.

George Rhodes, Spring Gove, Headingley, Leeds.

David Reid (Petrie), commercial traveller.

James Buchanan, Fellow of Peterhouse College, Cambridge.

Rowland Ewart, driver of the express, living at Gateshead (taken to Thirsk Hospital).

Edward Head, fireman of the express, living at Gateshead.

Sources:

Huddersfield Daily Examiner 1892

Leeds Mercury 1892

Coroner's Inquest documents Ref C3/1/1 (1892/86)

Part 4

Design Faults

17

Sheffield Flood

Sheffield

1864

The year 2007 was disastrous for South Yorkshire. Floods devastated the areas around Rotherham, Barnsley and Sheffield, causing misery for businesses and homeowners alike. A number of people lost their lives in the appalling conditions. But this was the force of Nature, for which no one can fully prepare. Almost 150 years previously a flood that owed more to Man's intervention than to natural hazards devastated the area.

The River Loxley flows down the valleys above Sheffield through tiny villages including Malin Bridge, Hillsbrough and Owlerton before joining the River Don. It was in this area in 1859 that the Sheffield Waterworks Company decided to build its ninth huge reservoir.

*Damflask Reservoir, Sheffield which covers some of the area where the Bradfield
Reservoir flooded*

It was built on a massive scale, intended to hold around 691,000,000 gallons of water, primarily for the purpose of supplying water to the many factories and mills around Sheffield. The previous reservoirs had all been completed successfully but this last seems to have been flawed from the start and in 1864 the project went disastrously wrong. The Dale Dyke reservoir burst its banks.

The Water Company's engineer, John Gunson, heard the warning that stormy weather was expected and went to inspect the dam, but all appeared well. However, an hour or so later one of the workmen, William Horsefield, saw a small crack in the side of the embankment. Others were called to inspect the crack, including farmers from around the valley as well as Water Company employees, but no agreement was reached as to whether the crack was dangerous or not. By the time it was realised just how serious the situation was it was too late for warnings to be given. One of the men there, Jonathan Ibbotson, said:

'Language cannot convey any just description of the awful thundering, crashing roar of the torrent. It was as if the earth itself was being rent asunder by the impetuous stream ...'

The 'stream' followed the line of the River Loxley from Bradfield, destroying houses, factories and stone-built bridges that stood in its path. Most of the population were still in bed, and over 240 people perished.

Then, as now, the disaster brought out the best and the worst in people. Joseph Dawson, a tailor, of Lower Bradfield, was at home with his wife who had just given birth to their second child. Fortunately, Joseph's brother was staying with them and on realising what was happening, he was sent off to carry Joseph's eldest child to safety. Joseph tried to get help but a man nearby refused and left him to fend for himself. Joseph then tried to carry both his wife and day-old baby but was knocked over by flood. Though he managed to get back to the house, he was unable to keep hold of the baby, which became the flood's youngest victim. Joseph and his wife finally managed to get upstairs and out via the back window that was near the banking. Others were more generous with their help.

The waters continued down to Damflask, Malin Bridge, Owlerton, and Neepsend, through Sheffield, past Kelham Island and Rotherham before finally petering out in Doncaster. All along the route property had been ruined, roads and bridges wrecked and lives lost.

By Saturday 12 March, the *Sheffield Independent* was running vivid descriptions of the 'foaming, boiling river'. It is obvious that at that point, no one was sure what had happened, but the Sunday papers reported that already there was a 'multitude of visitors' flocking to the town to view the area, and the papers comment on the 'evils of industrialisation' and its need for a workforce, which then had to be supplied with coal and water. The *Sheffield Independent* stressed that it 'was not making an appeal' which it considered would be 'an affront' to its readers. They simply relied on their readers to 'come forward at once with the princely munificence and Christian kindness which they have so often shown.' A few days later, they were publishing lists of subscribers. Many were from businesses in the area, but there were also many individual donations and all are named, together with the amount given, ranging from £500 from George Hadfield MP to £1 from Rev C S Enright. A public meeting was called; again the leading citizens making this demand were listed in the paper, as were those responding to the appeal by making donations. In the event, not all of this money was distributed. Some was returned to the donors if known, whilst the rest was given to other charities.

Inquests had to be held after sudden deaths and these generally took place almost immediately after the death. Though coroner's reports rarely survive, the details can be found in the newspapers. The first inquest was on eighty-six bodies, each one viewed by the jurors: Henry Pawson (foreman), John Prideaux, J B Fordham, John Walker, C J Porter, Henry Pearce, Thomas Appleyard, John Howson, John Bland, R Booth, S Dawson, F W Colley, Thomas Cole, Frederick Mercer, Edward Bennet, William Marples. There were so many bodies that evidence of identification was only taken for a few before the inquest was adjourned, for example, Thomas and Elizabeth Elston were identified by Henry Wragg of Sheffield, cutler and Keziah Heaton (or Eaton) was identified by Mary Ann Heaton, her brother-in-law's wife.

Over the weeks following the flood, small advertisements began to appear – appeals for information about missing persons, often with a description and contact addresses or details of items found amongst the debris. Not everyone was honest though. On 15 March there appeared details of Samuel Gould who was caught and convicted of stealing bars of steel that he had 'found' near his home. Gradually a list of those missing, where they had lived, when and where their bodies had been found and where they were interred was put together. According to Samuel Harrison who was a reporter in Sheffield at the time and wrote a vivid description of the events, almost thirty bodies were never recovered and thirty-five were buried without being identified. Some bodies were washed a considerable distance or were not found for many weeks after the event. Many others who survived the actual flood, died later from injuries or disease.

The newspapers gave what details they had at the time. There is a reference to 'Widow Hatchell of Malin Bridge who kept a school' who drowned and 'Mr Gray who had a trotter shop' which was gutted. They also comment on one man that: 'We could not ascertain his name any further than that he went by the alias of William Bethney and he came from Masbro' – he is possibly later listed as William Bethel.

Many are mentioned in daring rescues and since the flood took place just three years after a census year it is possible to find the families before the destruction took place. Henry Porton had arrived in Sheffield from Lancashire some seven years earlier making a living for himself in the steel industry. He not only saved his wife, Ann, sons George, Henry, and Joe, and daughters Janet and Jane but also went out into the floods to rescue his neighbour's little girl. Next he went out to rescue the Howard family, brought them into his own house and went back again for the Fletchers and their three children. At Bacon Island James Sharman was roused by the local policeman, John Thorpe, and was able to save his family including his wife, Mary, daughter, two daughters-in-law and four grandchildren. The census details tell us that James, a blacksmith, came from Worksop in Nottinghamshire, whilst the rest of this family were from Sheffield. His daughter, Emma, would have been eighteen at the time of the flood and his two sons, James and Edwin, would have been twenty-three and twenty respectively – quite young to be married with families. The census also shows that his mother-in-law, Mary Oldham, had been living with them though she had probably died by the time of the flood. The policeman who gave the alarm was eventually promoted and given a small financial reward by the Watch Committee, like many other policemen who were highly commended for their part in the rescue operation.

The survivors generally lost everything; often even the 'shirt on their backs' was torn from them by the floodwaters. A committee dealt with claims for compensation and their records can still be seen at the archives in Sheffield. Some manufacturers claimed for the loss of their buildings, stock or work lost, for example claim number 1425 from William Knight, cutler at 8 Cross Church Street, was for loss of wages for himself at 4 shilling a day, two able men at 3 shillings a day and one boy at one shilling and sixpence a day. He was given £1 14s 6d in total.

Others put in much longer claims and give a good idea of their lifestyle. Claim number 2232 was from Sarah Knight a widow living at 41 Russell Street. She lists all the items lost from her house including three chairs and a table valued at 12s 6d, four beer bottles at 3s 6d, fender and irons, for the fireside, at 3s and clothing valued at £1. An item that we won't see nowadays was a 'winder edge' valued at 1s 6d. This could have been a cloth covering the bottom of the window. Her house must have survived because she put in a claim for cleaning it – £3. However, the committee rarely seem to have granted the full amounts. Sarah's total claim came to £9 18s 6d but she was awarded less than a third of this. Samuel Marshall, a scythe and sickle man-ufacturer at Globe Works, claimed over £40 for his personal property and stock-in-trade losses and was awarded almost ninety per cent of the value.

The principal cemeteries used were at Bradfield, Burngreave, General Cemetery, Loxley Chapel, Rivelin Glen, St John's Park, Sheffield, Stannington and Wadsley. A number have gravestones that refer to the events of the flood and some name those whose body was never recovered. As other members of the family may also be listed, these are a useful source of information, but may need careful interpretation. According to the list of dead, John King, twenty-five, was buried in 'Sheffield' Cemetery, which could mean the General Cemetery. However, according to the gravestone of his parents, John King, a police constable of Sheffield, he is buried in Burngreave Cemetery. Other physical reminders of the event can be found at St Polycarp's church, Malin Bridge where there is a plaque to those from the local area and two stone memorials in Bradfield to mark the position of the original dam.

These details give the name, age, and place of residence of those who died:

Buried at Attercliffe: Thomas Gill, forty-eight, Attercliffe.

Buried at Barmby Dun: Charles Broughton, twenty-three, Malin Bridge.

Buried at Bradfield: Henry Burkinshaw, thirty-six, Loxley; the Crapper family of Malin Bridge: Joseph, forty-four, Elizabeth, forty, Joseph jnr, fourteen; baby Dawson, two days, Low Bradfield; Stephen Ibbotson, twenty, Loxley; Thomas Kay, seventy, Malin Bridge; William Longley, forty, Loxley; the whole of the Trickett family of Malin Bridge were buried together: James, forty, Elizabeth, thirty-four, Jemima, thirteen and James, six.

Buried at Burngreave Cemetery: William Bonser, sixty-two, Allen Street; Ann Cook, eighty-seven, Rutland Road; John Eaton, forty-nine, Kelham Island; Keziah Eaton, fifty-one, Kelham Island; Thomas Elston, thirty, Neepsend; Elizabeth Green, fifty-three, Harvest Lane; Richard Hazelhurst, seventy-eight,

Gravestone of John King

Joiner Lane; Alfred Hukin, forty-five, Neepsend Gardens; Sarah Hukin, forty-five, Neepsend Gardens; Annis Jackson, twelve, Neepsend Gardens; George Mills, sixty-two, Hill Bridge; Hannah Mills, fifty-eight, Hill Bridge; Martha Needham, two, Neepsend Lane; Edward Riley, thirty-eight, Hillfoot; Emma Sparkes, twenty-seven, Harvest Lane; Alfred Sparkes, five, Harvest Lane; Emma Sparkes, three months, Harvest Lane; Jonathan Turner, seventeen, Nursery Lane; Sidney James Varney, eighteen, Kelham Street; John Vaughan, sixty-four, Harvest lane; Elizabeth Vaughan, fifty-three, Harvest Lane; Peter Webster, thirty, Neepsend Gardens; Sarah Webster, thirty, Neepsend Gardens; Robert Webster, three years six months, Neepsend Gardens; Peter Webster, one year six months, Neepsend Gardens; Priscilla Willett, sixteen, Long Croft.

Buried at Loxley Chapel:
From Malin Bridge: Eliza Armitage, sixty-four, William Armitage, thirty-seven, Ann Armitage, forty, Charles Armitage, twelve, William Armitage, four, Greaves Armitage, twenty-eight, Sarah Armitage, thirty, Thomas Bates, forty-two, Harriet Bates, forty, George Bates, nineteen, Thomas Bates, ten.

Burngreave Cemetery where many victims were buried

From Little Matlock: Daniel Chapman, thirty-two, Ellen Chapman, thirty, Samuel Chapman, three, Frederick Chapman, six, William Chapman, fourteen, Alathea Hague, seventeen.
From Old Wheel: Joseph Denton, sixteen.

Buried at Owlerton:
From Malin Bridge: Thomas Bullard, forty and Sarah Ann Bullard, thirty-seven.

Buried at Doncaster:
A servant man, seventeen, of Malin Bridge.

Buried at Fulwood:
William Simpson, thirty-six, of Hillfoot.

Buried at General Cemetery:
From Neepsend Lane: Catherine Albert, twenty-five, John Albert, five, Mary Jane Albert, ten months, Mary Bright, fifty-seven, Eliza Bright, four, Alfred Bright, twelve, Mary Bright, seven, Thomas Fairest, forty-seven, John Needham, four, Jane Peters, eight, Julia Peters, four, Christopher Peters, two.

From Neepsend:
Alfred Coggan, thirteen, Eliza Coggan, eight, William Coggan, six, Elizabeth Elston, thirty, Thomas Elston, two weeks, John Gannon, thirty-six, Sarah Gannon, thirty, Peter Gannon, five years six months, Henry Gannon, eleven, William Gannon, four, John Gannon, nine, Margaret Gannon, four months.

From Neepsend Gardens: Susannah Gilyett, fifty-three, John Midwood, forty-six, Phoebe Midwood, thirty-seven, George Midwood, eight.

From Hillsborough: John C Appleby, thirty-two, Mary Appleby, sixty-three, Mary Appleby, thirteen.

From Long Croft: Christopher B Arculus, nine, Christopher Colton, thirty-two, Mary Colton, thirty.

From Hill Bridge: Eliza Mappin, fifty, Sarah Ann Pickering, twenty-four, Elizabeth Pickering, twenty-four, Mary Snape, forty-four.

From Owlerton: John Turton, sixty, Susannah Turton, seventy-three. Emma Wallis, forty-seven, Cotton Mill Row; George Snape, forty-two, Hillsborough; Richard Peacock, fifty-eight, Midland Depot.

Buried at Handsworth:
Joseph Barker, twenty-seven, Malin Bridge.

Buried at Heeley:
James Frith, thirty-two, Malin Bridge.

Buried at Kilnhurst:
Rebecca Wright, twenty-nine, Bacon Island.

Buried at Mortonley:
Marie Hill, eighteen, Malin Bridge

Buried at Rivelin Glen:
From Neepsend: Thomas Petty, forty, Margaret Petty, thirty-four, Mary Petty, eleven, Catherine Petty, seven, Thomas Petty, three.
Robert Ryder, eleven, Long Croft;
Dennis McLaughlin, seventy-four, Dun Street.

Buried at Sheffield Cemetery:
From Malin Bridge: Emma Barratt, twenty-six, Joseph Goddard, fifty-six, Sarah Goddard, fifty-four, John Hudson, forty, George Hudson, five, Isabella Jepson, twenty-seven, Jepson, eleven months, Caroline Watson, six, Sarah Ann Watson, thirty, George Watson, three, Mary Yeardley, twenty-eight.
John King, twenty-five, Loxley.
Herbert G Marshall, one, Hillsborough
Ann Pearson, forty-seven, Hillsborough.

Buried at St John's Park:
From Harvest Lane: Samuel Crump, thirty-eight, Mary Crump, seventy-one.
From Neepsend Lane: John Glover, twenty-five, Sarah Ann Glover, twenty-five;
From Neepsend: John Mayor, fifty-five, Elizabeth Mayor, fifty, Sarah Mayor, twenty-two.

Buried at St Mary's:
Christopher Colton, four, Long Croft.

Buried at Stannington:
From Malin Bridge: James Bagshaw, fifty-six, Mary Bagshaw, fifty-two, Walter Damms, twenty, Thomas Spooner, forty, Selina Spooner, forty, William Spooner, nineteen, Hannah Spooner, forty-eight, Jonathan Spooner, forty, Benjamin Spooner, seventy-six, Sarah Ann Spooner, seventy.

Buried at Thurgoland:
From Hillsborough: Joseph Dyson, thirty-four, Mary Dyson, thirty-two, Arthur Dyson, eleven, Priscilla Dyson, seven, James Dyson, five, Ann Dyson, three, Samuel Seynor, twenty-six, Richard Snape, seventeen.

Buried at Wadsley:
From Hillsborough: Morris Atkinson, forty-eight, William Atkinson, twelve, James Atkinson, forty-one, William Atkinson, forty-two, George Atkinson, eighteen, Isaac Turner, forty, Turner, forty-four, Jonathan Ibbotson, nine.
From Malin Bridge: George Bisby, forty-four, Ann Mount, forty-one, Charles Price, fifty, Elizabeth Price, fifty, Sarah Price, twenty-eight, Charles J Price, two, Price, two days. William Sellars, fifty-two, Caroline Sellars, forty-eight, Charlotte Taylor, forty-five, William Wolstenholme, seventy-two.
Joseph Gregory, twenty, Little Matlock.
Charles Platts, thirty-four, Loxley.

Buried at Walkley:
William Crookes, twenty-six, Hill Bridge

Buried at Wardsend:
Joseph Dean, seventeen, Owlerton.
From Barracks: Isabella Foulds, five, John Foulds, three.

The records do not show the place of burial of the following:
From Malin Bridge: Elizabeth Crownshaw, seventeen, John Hawksley, sixty-one, George Tingle, thirty-two, Samuel Armitage, seven, Henry Armitage, ten, Maria Armitage, one year nine months, Mary Armitage, four, Elizabeth Armitage, three months, George Barratt, twenty-eight, William Barratt, two, Walter Bates, seventeen, Sarah Bisby, forty-three, Teresa Bisby, fourteen, Elizabeth Bisby, twelve, Thomas Bisby, nine, Hannah Bisby, six, Hugh Bisby, four, Etches, seventy, Henry Hall, thirty-eight, Elizabeth Hudson, thirty-nine, Mary Hudson, ten, George Jepson, seventy, George Jepson, sixty-eight, Sarah Longley, twenty-six, Mary Longley, four, Jane Ann Longley, one year six months, Edward Price, twenty-five, Frederick Spooner, fifteen, Thomas Spooner, eight, Mary Ann Spooner, ten, Betty Spooner, six, Albert Spooner, four, Henry Spooner, two, George Trickett, four, Rosina Yeardley, three, John Yeardley, two, a servant girl, eighteen
Thomas Winter, seventy, Owlerton.

From Hillsborough:
Sarah Atkinson, fifteen, Robert Atkinson, twenty, Sophia Dyson, thirteen, George Radford, thirty, Elizabeth Radford, twenty-eight, John Radford, seven, Isaac Turner, fourteen, Sarah Ann Turner, ten, William Waters, twenty-two.

From Little Matlock:
Walter Booth, sixteen, John Bower, seventeen, George Clay, fifteen.

From Bacon Island:
Mary C Johnson, nine, George Wright, thirty-three.

From Hill Bridge:
Thomas Merryman, twenty-three, William Pickering, twenty-four.

From Neepsend Gardens:
Dawson Midwood, sixteen, Fanny Midwood, four.
William Bethel, thirty-two, Limerick Wheel.
William Bradbury, twenty-eight, Rowell Bridge.
Edward Cross, fourteen, Neepsend Lane.
Sarah Ann Gannon, two, Neepsend.

Sources:
A complete History of the Great Flood at Sheffield, Samuel Harrison (ISBN 0 904293 01 7)
Collapse of the Dale Dyke Dam 1864, Geoffrey Amey (ISBN 0 304293 62 8).

Index of Claimants for Sheffield Flood 1864 ref: 1998/72 in Sheffield Archives.
There is a project underway at the moment under the auspices of Sheffield Hallam University to digitise the claims registers and make the information available online
www.shef.ac.uk/misc/personal/cs1ma/flood/flood.html"
(excellent website giving full details and photographs.)
http://freepages.genealogy.rootsweb.com/~engsheffield/k_lightowler/a_lightowler.htm another
(website with details of some of the families who died.)
www.bradfieldparish.org.uk/
(local history and details of walks around the Damflask area.)
1861 Census records.
Watch Committee Minutes, Sheffield Archives.
Sheffield Daily Telegraph 1861

18

R38 Airship Disaster

Hull

1921

'The brave aviators faced their inevitable fate alone, faced it like men and heroes.'
Hull Daily Mail, 26 August 1921

At 695 feet long, she was the world's largest airship, longer than York Minster. It seemed almost ethereal. Slender aluminium buttresses, thin-looking wires to support the duckboard that provided a passageway along the length of the ship. The cabin in which crew and passengers sat had walls barely as thick as a tent:

> *'A strong kick and your foot is through the sides. It is like a paper house,' stated the* Huddersfield Daily Examiner, *'yet everything is exactly calculated and its strength is more than adequate.'*

Powered by six engines and reaching a top speed of 71 miles per hour, everyone was looking forward to the final tests.

The *R38* had been made at the Royal Airship Works at Cardington, Bedfordshire. Originally planned for patrolling the North Sea and protecting ships, the project had been abandoned at the end of World War One but it was finally agreed to sell the ship to the USA and provide training for their crew. A hangar, large enough to take two ships the size of the *Mauritania*, had been built in New Jersey ready for the *R38* – renamed by the US as *ZR2*. In June 1921, the *R38* was

AIRSHIP DISASTER.

R38 COLLAPSES AND FALLS INTO THE HUMBER.

HALIFAX MAN AMONG THE FIVE SURVIVORS.

Headline, Hull Advertiser

ready to transfer to the airship base near Howden for a series of final trials. Minor damage was done to some girders on this transfer flight and comments were made then about strength having been sacrificed for lightness but these seem to have been ignored.

The new airship was already painted in US colours and renamed the *ZR2*. By August the ship was ready to show what it could do. Captain Little brought the ship out of the shed at Howden where the complex included mammoth sheds, a gas-making plant, electricity works and quarters for officers and men. There also, outside the sheds, could be seen the remains of the *R34*, which had previously flown to America and back before being wrecked whilst trying to re-house her in the shed.

Sixteen Americans were on board *R38*, together with thirty-three British personnel who were responsible for flying the craft. Included were representatives from the National Physical Laboratory which had been established in 1900 to 'promote links between science and commerce', setting standards for physical measurements such as time, length, mass, density and force. On Wednesday 24 August, the ship left Howden, flying low over the surrounding countryside and out across Hull and the River Humber:

'The heavy throbbing of her six three hundred and fifty horse-power engines, unusually loud in the quiet early morning drew people to bedroom windows or out of doors. They were rewarded by a fine sight for the airship could be observed sailing majestically through the fog which hung at low altitude...'

The *Hull Daily Mail* enthusiastically described the ship's passing overhead with pride in the achievement. The ship was taking part in an extensive thirty hours trial and then going straight on to Pulham in Norfolk before setting out for America, commanded by her new US Navy crew. Hull people did not expect to see the ship return.

The trials took place as expected, at various altitudes and a variety of speeds but as the ship approached Norfolk, fog covered the airship station and it was agreed that instead of docking, the ship would spend the night over the North Sea. Heavy thunderstorms passed over the area but the airship 'behaved admirably'. In the morning the airfield was still obscured by thick fog however so it was decided to return to Howden, carrying out more trials en route. At half past four the captain sent a message to base 'carrying out full speed trials' and, indeed, took the ship successfully to over 71 mph.

At five o'clock he signalled that he was returning to Howden, expecting to reach there by half past six. Half an hour later, they sailed across the coast and were over Hull once more. The ship suddenly dipped lower and the watching inhabitants thought it was going to fly lower to give them all chance to see it better. Thousands were in the vicinity as they returned home from their day's work, thronging the streets to watch the colossal airship.

Unbelievably the back of the ship began to crumple up in the middle. Witnesses said they thought there was a sudden burst of speed and a 'lightning dash' out over Victoria Pier as if the commander had realised what was happening and raced for the river away from the town. Moments later the ship broke in two, dropped into the river and exploded in flames, terrifying the people nearby who still had vivid memories of the bombing in the recent war, and shattering windows along the riverside.

Tugs in the area swiftly put out to find any survivors. Whilst most of it was seriously damaged in the explosion, the tailpiece was intact and some survivors were plucked to safety. The tug 'Englishman' quickly returned with Captain Wann, a blood-soaked handkerchief over his face. He was rushed to the Royal Infirmary. Widespread cheering then broke out as the tug, Norman, brought back a young man alive. As bodies were recovered, they were taken to the Great Central Station before being transferred to the mortuary.

One American airman, A C M Broom, had a very lucky escape. He was due to go on board at Howden but arrived just two minutes late and was left behind, but later went to Hull to watch the ship pass overhead and saw the crash. He was one of the first to clamber on to the wreck seeking his missing comrades.

In London, rumours quickly spread and relatives of the crew descended on the Air Ministry for news. 'In due time officials disclosed to them as tactfully as possible the news that those whose fate was their intimate concern were among 'those unaccounted for…''

Over the next few days searches for more bodies were made along the banks of the river. Officials went out to the wreck, which could be reached at low tide, but salvage required a floating crane to be brought in to lift the heavy wreckage.

An American officer, who was on the salvage boat when the body of Air Commodore Maitland was found, said that he still 'had his hand on the control cord' and the American commented that 'the gallant officer had died like a hero'.

When C I R Campbell, the designer and superintendent of the Royal Air Works, was found, it was discovered that his watch had stopped at 5.50. It was said of him that 'he had died the death he would have chosen'.

The Americans in Britain held a supplementary inquiry into the loss of personnel, reporting to their Navy Department in addition to the inquests into the deaths in Hull and the Air Ministry conducted a Court of Inquiry at the Howden Airship base under the control of Air Vice Admiral Sir John Salmond. Other members of the team included Air Commodore F R Scarlet, Group Captain A M Longmore, Group Captain A B Burdett, Wing Commander H M Cave Browne-Cave and Squadron Leader R B B

Colmore. The US Naval Attaché was also invited to appoint a representative to attend.

Gradually the story began to be pieced together. Flight Lieutenant Wann was able to make a statement from the hospital explaining that it all happened in five seconds. The ship had run beautifully at sixty knots and had reduced speed to fifty when suddenly there was a violent crack. He thought some of the girders had broken and then the explosions followed:

'I saw several of them leap into space and I went down with the vessel until near the water's edge when I jumped, but got entangled.'

He remembered nothing more until he woke up in hospital, though he was quick to stress that he was in sole charge of the ship, ensuring no one else would be blamed, whatever the outcome of the inquiry. He felt the accident occurred because of weak structural parts, which caused the ship to break in two, though he could not say which parts:

'I had been flying for thirty-six hours before the mishap occurred and I intended to make that my last flight.'

Harry Bateman, Scientific Assistant from the National Physical Laboratory, who was in the tail taking photographs of the pressure on the fins, noticed that the speed dropped:

'I heard from Major Pritchard that the controls were going to be moved fairly rapidly in order to afford a severe test as to the airworthiness of the ship to cross the Atlantic.'

He noticed the designer and Air Commodore Maitland looking round the ship for defects and the speed was reduced to fifty knots. After this the ship seemed to be shaken about, the girders cracked and the tail fell. Bateman was thrown into the cockpit where he grabbed a parachute and jumped. The tape from the parachute harness got entangled in some gear and he was left dangling over the side of the ship until rescue arrived. His opinion was that in carrying out rudder tests at high speed, too great a strain was imposed on the ship when she suddenly swung round on to a south-westerly course as she approached the Humber from the north.

The airship fell, tail up, into the water. Wireless Officer Welch stayed at his post to the last, sending the final message to Howden that the ship was breaking and falling.

It was pointed out at the inquiry that this was an accident that had occurred during a trial trip of an experimental airship:

*'I do not think that it is a proof that airships are necessarily dangerous and
therefore they are no good.'*

commented Major General Sir W S Brancker. The government, at least, did
not seem to agree with this view since by October it was announced that the
sheds in Howden were to be closed and all work on airships stopped.

The official report cites 'structural weakness' as the cause of the crash
attributed to a lack of vital information. Specifically it comments that many
new features were introduced in the design but it appeared that there was a
lack of 'vital aero-dynamical information' as to the effect of these modifica-
tions on the strength of the structure. The Board of Enquiry failed to give any
technical opinions.

The final inquest on thirty-three of the victims was held on 5 October in
the Guildhall in Hull before Dr T C Jackson, deputy coroner. He asked the
jury to consider whether any negligence had occurred and to consider what
precautions could be taken to prevent an occurrence of a similar tragedy.
Engineers, designers and naval personnel, including Flight Lieutenant Little
of US Navy and Albert Edward Gerrish, works manager of the Royal Airship
Works in Bedford, described the construction and testing of the airship,

Guildhall, Hull

stressing the successful trials that had taken place and the alterations that had been made to improve the ship. A gasbag test as early as May 1920 had showed up signs of weakness in the transverse girders but this was rectified. Again in June 1921 a transverse girder had given way when an inspector had knelt on it. But this had been replaced. On 17 July a long flight had taken place with Mr Campbell the designer on board. In severe tests two girders had buckled on the port side but this was believed to be due to wind pressure from the forward propeller impinging on the fabric of the airship and forcing the girders inward. All parts showing stress were promptly renewed and strengthened. The girders were double braced and a further trial flight proved satisfactory. Turning tests were also carried out; though they showed up a tendency for the rudder to go over on some occasions this was not considered important. Harold Wyn Evans for the Royal Corps of Naval Constructors stated that he had experience of airships going back to the first rigid airship to fly – the *R9* and the *R38* had carried out her trials with less trouble than any predecessors.

Wann had still not recovered sufficiently to be able to attend and the jury pointed out that although they'd heard all about the tests they had not heard from the man carrying them out. They asked for a further adjournment but the coroner dissuaded them. Any adjournment would have to be a very long one and since Wann remembered nothing of the accident it was felt that he could, in the end, contribute nothing further to the inquest. The jury ultimately agreed to retire and eventually brought in a verdict of accidental death due to the airship breaking due to some cause or causes unknown.

Of the forty-nine people on board, only five people survived the crash – Harry Bateman, of Halifax, from the National Physical Laboratory; Flight Lieutenant A H Wann, captain of the ship; Leading Aircraftman E W Davis; Corporal W P Potter; and Commander Walker, an American.

British victims:
Air Commander Edward M Maitland, commander of the airship base at Howden.
Flight Lieutenant I C Little.
Flight Lieutenant Rupert S Montagu, navigator.
Flying Officer Thomas F Mathewson, engineering officer, from Barnby.
C I R Campbell, Superintendent of the Royal Air Works.
F Warren, Royal Air Ship Works and assistant constructor of the airship.
John Rye.
William Oliver, from Sheffield.
John W Wilson, from York.

All the above are buried under the memorial in Western Cemetery, Hull.

Memorial to the victims of the R38 crash, Hull

J R Pannell, of National Physical Laboratory.
C W Duffield, of National Physical Laboratory.
Flight Lieutenant G M Thomas.
Flying Officer Victor H Wicks.
Flight Lieutenant J E M Pritchard, Air Ministry representative.
S J Heath.
William H Greener.
Harold Thompson.
Frank Smith, of Halifax.
Alfred T Martin.
Charles W Penson.
J W Mason.
Frederick W Burton.
G S Anger.
John C Drew.
C W Donald.
Roy Parker.
E E Steere.
R Withington.

Americans:
Commander L A Maxfield.
Lieutenant Commander W N Bieg.
Lieutenant Commander H W Hoyt.
Lieutenant Commander G G Little.
Lieutenant Commander M H Esterley.
Lieutenant Commander E W Coil.
John Truscott Hancock.
L E Crowl.
A L Loftin.
W A Julius.
G Welch.
C J Aller.
R M Coons.
W J Steele.
A D Pettit.
M Lay.

On 1 September, a memorial service was held at Holy Trinity church in Hull where the congregation overflowed onto the surrounding streets. All the civic

Holy Trinity Church, Hull

dignitaries attended as did the American consul and representatives from all the Services. The procession wound its way from the Guildhall to the church whilst shops closed and British and American flags flew at half-mast on many buildings.

Equally huge crowds turned out to watch the departure of the American victims from Hull docks. The fifteen caskets, each draped with an American flag and covered in flowers. A procession was led by the band of the 1st West Yorkshire Regiment with detachments for the RAF and US Navy.

On 7 September a memorial service was held in Westminster Abbey, London.

Many of bodies of the Americans were returned to the United States on board British light cruiser *Dauntless* as a mark of respect.

Sources:
www.roll-of-honour.com/Yorkshire/HullR38Memorial.html
http://www.airshiponline.com/airships/r38/index.html
Hull Daily Mail 1921

The memorial in Western Cemetery, Hull has brass plaques on either side, commemorating the British and the American losses. In May 2007 the cemetery suffered considerable vandalism resulting in damage to many stones and the loss of the plaque containing the names of all the British victims. In the centre of the memorial, the inscription reads:

> TO THE GLORY OF GOD
> AND IN MEMORY OF
> OFFICERS AND MEN OF
> THE ROYAL AIR FORCE
> AND OF THE
> RIGID AIR DETACHMENT
> UNITED STATES NAVY
> MEMBERS OF THE STAFF OF
> THE NATIONAL PHYSICAL
> LABORATORY AND OF THE
> ROYAL AIRSHIP WORKS
> LOST IN THE R38 (ZR2)
> AUGUST 24TH 1921

Part 5

War

19

An Early Yorkshire Disaster

1069

O ne date that everyone is expected to know is probably 1066 – a pivotal date in English history. But how many people would be able to answer if you asked: 'What was the major event in Yorkshire in 1069?'

There has always been a 'north/south divide' in England. Even in the Anglo-Saxon period, the lands north of the Humber were seen as separate, wild and strange, frequently attacked by the Scots, by the Danes and by Vikings. It was not until the seventh century that York developed as the ecclesiastical centre of the north, though Lindisfarne and Hexham further north were the more famous for another century.

Eventually throwing in their lot with the southern kings, Yorkshire was ruled by a succession of earls including Tostig, brother of Harold Godwinson, appointed in 1055. Ten years later, a 'gemote' or public judicial meeting deposed him and chose their own successor. Surprisingly they passed over Waltheof the son of Siward who had been a very popular earl, and elected Morcar the brother of Edwin, Earl of Mercia. King Edward soon ratified this appointment.

The following year King Edward died and was succeeded by King Harold (Godwinson) who visited York and issued coins minted in the city. In September 1066 Tostig, angered by his brother's lack of support, reappeared with Harold Hardrada of Norway, defeating Earl Morcar and Morcar's brother Edwin at Fulford. Though York immediately surrendered to Tostig and Hardrada, King Harold killed both men at Stamford Bridge a few days later, whilst King Harold himself was killed a few weeks later at Hastings. It was the end of an era for Yorkshire as well as England.

Very little was written about events at the time but Orderic Vitalis (1075 – c1142) was a Norman/English priest whilst Simeon of Durham was a monk in the north of England, both writing almost contemporary accounts of the times. The Anglo-Saxon Chronicles too were written soon after the events and all agree on the principal happenings.

Earls Edwin and Morcar promptly surrendered to the Conqueror, although William appointed Copsi, a Northumbrian who had originally supported Tostig but who had quickly changed sides and done homage to William. Osulf, son of the Earl of Bernicia who considered himself the heir to Northumbria, soon murdered Copsi. This too did not last long as Osulf was also swiftly murdered! William then sold the earldom to Earl Gospatrick and went off to concentrate his efforts on quelling the west country.

At this point Edgar the Aetheling, grandson of Edmund Ironside and the last of the Saxon royal line, rebelled against William and was joined by Gospatrick, Edwin, Earl of Mercia and Morcar, the deposed Earl of Northumbria. William marched north, starting castles at Nottingham and Lincoln. This so alarmed the northerners that the Aetheling fled to Scotland and York had no alternative but to surrender. William built the first castle in the city, probably on what is now Clifford's Tower area. Leaving 500 knights there, he marched south to set up castles at Lincoln, Huntingdon and Cambridge.

In 1068 William gave Northumberland to Robert de Comines who took a large army of around nine hundred men north. He arrived in Durham in

Clifford's Tower, York

January 1069 but in his arrogance, refused to listen to a warning from the bishop that a large English army was in the area. Early in the morning of 28 January he was attacked and burned to death inside his house whilst most of his men were killed in fighting. Soon afterwards Edgar Aetheling came down from Scotland, joined with the Northumbrians and marched to York where he was widely welcomed, except by the sheriff William Malet who reported to King William that if he had no assistance he would be driven to surrender. William marched with his usual rapidity from the south with a large army, slaughtering those who could not escape. The Anglo-Saxon Chronicle also says he:

> 'Plundered the borough and made St Peter's Church an object of scorn, and also plundered and humiliated all the others.'

Edgar went back again to Scotland. A second castle was then built in York before William set off to spend Easter in Winchester. Even then more rebels attacked the two castles, though William FitzOsbern quickly defeated them.

Early in September 1069 a Danish invasion fleet of two hundred and forty ships, led by three of the sons of King Swein together with Earl Esborn and Earl Thurkill arrived in the Humber, after having sailed up from Kent and raiding along the coast as they went. Soon the old leaders, Edgar, Gospatric, Waltheof and many others too hastened northward to join them. They were welcomed by York's citizens, but the Normans in the city promptly set fire to the houses near the castle, intending to prevent them being used to fill the moat, and enabling the attackers to reach the castle. Unfortunately, the flames spread, burning down most of the city and even the Minster itself. The Allies occupied the whole area and in the ensuing battle, most of the Normans were killed and the castles demolished. This event could have changed the whole course of history, but that the victors were more intent on collecting treasures, money and prisoners to take as slaves:

> 'When the king learned this, he marched northwards with all the levies he could muster and utterly laid waste that shire.' (Anglo-Saxon Chronicle)

The Danes went off to plunder Lincolnshire, but were chased north again by William himself. They were forced to flee across the Humber, out of William's reach. William had to leave Counts Robert of Mortain and Robert of Eu in charge watching the Danes whilst he went off to Stafford to quell the Mercian insurgents before then marching back to Yorkshire. At this point he was held up for three weeks at the crossing of the River Aire, at Taddensclyff, a town better known nowadays as Pontefract, somewhere near where the old Great North Road used to run. This is now an overgrown single file track, but you

Ralph's Cross, now known as the Stump Cross, Pontefract, at the side
of the old Great North Road

can still see the remains of the roadside Ralph's Cross (now known as Stump Cross since that is all that remains of it) which was certainly there by 1170 AD. The bridge was either broken or impassable, (though whether this was because of flooding or a deliberate act of rebellion giving rise to the future name of Pontefract or 'broken bridge' is mere conjecture), the river was in flood and the northern bank was held against him. The Danes reached York first, but William simply devastated the country around the city and prepared to starve them out. The Danes soon agreed to return to their ships and William apparently paid them to return to Denmark after wintering in the Humber.

Leaving a force to repair the castles, William then mercilessly 'harried the north', killing men, women and children, destroying whole villages and devastating the land to such an extent that those who survived the sword died later of starvation. Although the system of 'harrying' was a generally accepted strategy of war, involving taking hostages, mass deportation of the population, burning, looting and finally handing over the land to more loyal followers, contemporary writers all deplored William's actions as the most brutal ever witnessed, the priest Orderic Vitalis commenting that 'such barbarous homicide should not pass unpunished'. The dead were left lying in the fields where they had been killed as no one was left to bury them. Those who fled were left to starve and many had to go south to find food.

William returned to keep Christmas at York. Before he left in January however he agreed to the founding of Selby Abbey, the first Benedictine monastery founded in the north since the Conquest. Many believe this was prompted by William's conscience because of his actions. His conscience however did not stop him continuing his 'harrying' right up to the Tees, and from there across into Cheshire, Derbyshire, Shropshire and Staffordshire, nor did it stop him granting lands to a number of loyal followers who were encouraged to build castles from which they could govern, with whatever degree of brutality they liked. Alan 'the Red' held Richmond and built his castle on the hill above the River Swale and Ilbert de Lacy was given Pontefract, that same place which had held up William's march north the previous year. Motte and bailey castles were erected too at Middleham and Pickering, all soon to be replaced by solid stone.

Whilst the chroniclers may have exaggerated some of the accounts, William's own record of the value of his new country suggests that the land was destroyed in this way. In the Domesday book, written about twenty years later, half of the villages in the north riding and over one third in the east and west ridings are described as waste or part waste. 'Waste' may have been used for grazing rather than being cultivated, but it could have been because there was no-one there to cultivate it! Many villages had no population listed for them but no reason is given for this. It is possible that the remaining population were forcibly moved to other villages to provide a workforce. Some places show large areas of plough land but no or few teams of oxen to work it. This suggests that even after so many years, recovery was slow. For example, Long Marston had twenty-three plough lands but only four and a half plough teams. Its value in 1066 was £6 but by 1086 it was only worth

Norman doorway of Selby Abbey

just over £2. Many showed similar drops in value, though not all – 'while some showed an increase that was usually small, the great majority showed a decrease that was usually considerable.' (Darby and Maxwell). The records only show the values in 1066 and in 1087 when the surveyors arrived but in Cheshire the records give an intermediate date. These show a considerable drop in the value from the time Normans took over to Domesday suggesting

Richmond Castle

that the Harrying of the North was the prime cause of this devastation. It is logical to assume the same applied in Yorkshire.

The bulk of the devastation was on the Pennines, where hardly any village was left untouched, the land north of York and up to Northumbria, but also along the coast. Some of this destruction could have been because of the usual passage of an army, which fed 'off the land' but also to encourage the Danes to keep their bargain and go home. On the lowlands there was less damage done, suggesting that it was specific strongholds of the rebels that were targeted. It was also easier to keep control of flatter, more cultivated areas than the wild uplands. This suggests that the event was less of an army just left to run riot, than of a deliberate, controlled policy of extermination.

When William died in 1087, in Rouen, it is said that on his deathbed the only expression of remorse from him was for his actions in Yorkshire. Whether this was genuine remorse or genuine fear of his imminent interview with his Maker we shall never know:

'It was the most terrible visitation that had ever fallen on any large part of England since the Danish wars of Alfred's time.' (Stenton)

Sources:
Darby H C and Maxwell I S eds, *Domesday Geography of Northern England,* Cambridge University Press, 1962
Garmonsway, *The Anglo-Saxon Chronicle,* Dent & Sons, 1972
Rowley, Trevor *Norman England,* Batsford/English Heritage, 1997
Stenton, Sir Frank, *Anglo-Saxon England,* Oxford University Press, 1971

20

Barnbow Canaries

Leeds

1916

On 4 August 1914 Britain declared war on Germany and immediately began to mobilise troops. Women meanwhile armed themselves with knitting needles and produced socks by the dozen for the lads at the Front. It soon became clear that this was not enough and munitions factories sprang up all over the country – manned principally by women.

In September 1915 the National Filling Factory was opened at Barnbow, Leeds to undertake the work of filling shells, cartridges and components. Over 130,000 people applied for jobs in the factory but only 16,000 were actually employed, receiving a wage of £1 8s per week. Thirty-eight special trains brought the workers to Barnbow's own station from surrounding areas, with three shifts working round the clock. By December that year, the first output of munitions was on its way to the Front. Shortly after this a bonus scheme was introduced and production trebled. The wages went up even more, with many of the women earning over £10 per week, which was a massive sum for those days. It was some compensation for the fact that the chemicals used turned the workers' skin bright yellow and munitions workers were soon known throughout the country as 'Canaries'.

Working conditions were appalling. Ordinary clothing was not allowed so workers had to strip to their underwear before donning buttonless smocks and caps. Shoes had to be rubber-soled. The women could not have hairpins or combs, and certainly not cigarettes or matches. The air was hot and full of dust which caught in their throats and they worked an eight hour shift every day, six days a week. On Sundays there was no rest but twelve hour shifts were worked, with one Sunday off every three weeks. No one had a holiday.

The only advantage, apart from the wage, was that the girls were allowed to drink as much barley water and milk as they wished, because of the dreadful conditions. The factory had its own farm that produced 300 gallons of milk every day.

In Room 42 almost 200 women and girls worked, finishing the four and a half inch shells, which had already been loaded with high explosives. The fuse was inserted and the cap screwed down by hand. The shell was then taken to a machine that completed the task by screwing the cap down more tightly.

On Tuesday, 15 December 1916 the night shift started their work on the shells as normal. At 10.27pm there was a violent explosion which blew the room apart, fracturing the steam pipes which burst open and within seconds the floor was a slippery mixture of water and blood.

Ignoring the obvious danger, men and women ran into Room 42 to drag the injured to safety. William Parkin, a mechanic, was considered a hero, going back time and time again and rescuing at least a dozen girls. Later the girls put together and presented him with an inscribed silver watch for his bravery.

The injured were taken to the infirmary, where over the next few days, more girls died. The final total was thirty-five dead. The Barnbow Comfort Fund leased Weetwood Grange and those who survived were taken there to convalesce.

However, this was wartime and little of this event appears in the local papers of the time. The *Leeds Mercury* referred simply to an 'Explosion in a Northern Factory' where the workers displayed 'splendid bravery'. The Ministry of Munitions did acknowledge the courage and dedication of the workers:

> *'Prompt and effective steps were taken to deal with the emergency and the damage done to the factory was slight. The great majority of the workers in the factory are women and their behaviour is deserving of the highest praise.*
>
> *They displayed the greatest coolness and perfect discipline both in helping remove the injured and in continuing to carry on the work of the factory in spite of the explosion. The effect of the accident on the output of munitions will be negligible.'*

The Ministry were quite right to comment on the women's dedication. The injured, the dead and the debris were rapidly cleared from the area and the factory back to full production before the end of the shift.

An inquest was held on the victims who had died in the infirmary. In fact, two inquests were held – one by the West Riding Coroner and another by the Leeds City Coroner, though the latter were directed to follow the verdict of the first inquest so as to avoid unnecessary delay. At the West Riding inquest, after the coroner had expressed sympathy with the relatives, the solicitor who was representing the Board of Directors of the factory said:

> *'It would no doubt be some solace to the relatives to know that the victims*

died in the service of their country.'

The Board also admitted liability for compensation and varying amounts were paid out to surviving relatives. It was also announced at the inquest that a letter had been received from the Ministry of Munitions deploring the loss of life and 'admiring the pluck of the women engaged at the factory'. It went on to say that the Ministry would

> *'ask Sir Douglas Haig to let the men at the Front know of the courage and spirit which animated the womenfolk at home'.*

This was, in fact, done when Haig issued a special order of the day praising the 'British women who are working with us for a common cause.'

The coroner said that: 'It had been found impossible to arrive at the exact cause of the explosion' but it was probably some defect such as a shell exploding when the cap was screwed down too tightly or possibly a detonator protruding into the shell probably caused the explosion. The final verdict was: 'Death from shock owing to injury to vital organs caused accidentally by an explosion.'

In many cases, only the identification tags they were wearing enabled those who died to be named – the bodies were so badly mutilated no other means of identification was possible. The victims were generally taken home to be buried in their local cemetery.

From Leeds:
M Alderson.
Elsie Martha Atkinson, eighteen, daughter of Annie and John (deceased). Buried in Burmantofts Cemetery.
K Bainbridge.
Mary Jane Blackstone, thirty-five, wife of Arthur. Buried in Holbeck Cemetery.
Katie Chapman, forty-one, wife of John William. Buried in Woodhouse Cemetery.
Ethel Agnes Jackson. Buried Whitkirk Cemetery.
Emmie Keyworth, twenty-six, third daughter of Thomas and Eliza. Buried Lawnswood Cemetery.

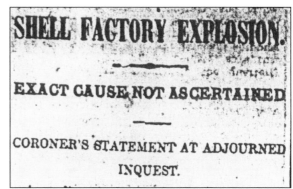

SHELL FACTORY EXPLOSION.

EXACT CAUSE NOT ASCERTAINED

CORONER'S STATEMENT AT ADJOURNED INQUEST.

Headline, Yorkshire Evening Press

Agnes L Power.
Gertrude Reid.
Mary Amelia Schofield, forty-two. Buried Chapeltown Old Cemetery.
Amelia Stewart.
Edith Sykes, who would shortly have celebrated her sixteenth birthday.
Florence Whitley, thirty-one, daughter of J E Naylor the widow of Ambrose
Whitley. Buried New Wortley Cemetery.
Ida Worslop.

From Pontefract:
Eleanor (often given as Helena) Beckett, thirty-nine.
Jane Few nee Handley. She was only twenty and had been married just five
weeks. Her husband, Charles, had returned to England to recuperate from
wounds so they had decided to get married before he returned to the Front.
Normally Jane would have given up work on marriage but munitions work
was so vital, she continued with her job. The family were well known in
Pontefract and the funeral was well attended by many in the area.

From Harrogate:
Emily Sedgwick.
Ada Glasby.
Olive Yeates, seventeen. Buried Grove Road Cemetery.

From Kippax:
Maggie Barker.

From Halton:
Maria Evelyn Rowley, nineteen, daughter of Frederick. Buried New Wortley
Cemetery.

From Normanton:
Jennie Blackamore.

From Castleford:
Mary Gibson, who was just fourteen years old.
Polly Booth, twenty-one.
Eliza Grant, forty, wife of Dixon Grant. Buried Allerton Bywater.
Edith Selena Levitt, tweny-nine. Buried Allerton Bywater.

From York:
Kathleen Violet Eastman, seventeen.
May Elizabeth Wortley, thirty-eight. She had ten children, seven under

fourteen years of age. The eldest was serving at the Front when she died, but all the others attended her funeral.

Mary Elizabeth Carter, twenty-two, who left a widower and a small child of two.

Elizabeth Mason, forty-one.

Lilian Eva Ellis, nineteen. The family had moved from Thirsk to York when her father joined the York City Police Force at the beginning of the war.

Eliza West, fifty-three.

All the above are buried in a communal grave in York.

Alice Smart.
Sarah Ann Jennings.
Charlotte Fox.
Olive Yeates.

The directors of the factory sent wreaths for all the victims and workers from the factory attended the funerals, often carrying the coffin of their deceased friends.

Memorial stone at Crossgates, Leeds

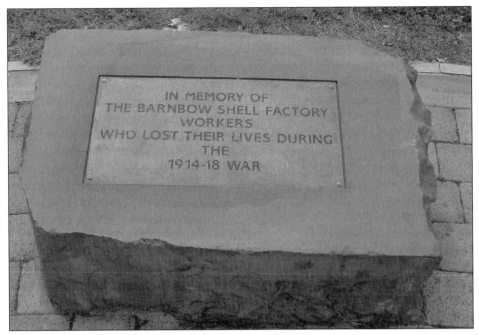

Centre memorial stone detail

There are a number of memorials to these victims. In Cross Gates, Leeds there is a stone memorial dedicated to all those who lost their lives in the munitions factory (there were two further explosions – in March 1917 and May 1918). Around the granite stones are a series of small plaques, each bearing the name of one of those who lost their life.

In York, the communal grave now has a memorial stone (thanks to the stonemason who provided this at his own expense), inscribed with the names of the six buried there, but also in the Minster is a memorial to all those women and girls who gave their lives during the war. You will, however, need to search diligently if you wish to see it. Head for the RAF Memorial Clock which is in a prominent position and just to the right you will see a series of wooden panels. Open them and behind is a list of all the 'women of Empire' who died.

The 'Five Sisters' window in the Minster, which has some extremely old glass in it, was re-dedicated on 24 June 1925 by the then Duchess of York, to the 1,400 women from all around the Empire who died whilst undertaking 'war work'.

After the war, the factory was used as an Army surplus store but in 1933 the buildings were dismantled. During World War Two an ordnance factory was built on the site.

Memorial stone, York Cemetery

Sources:
Yorkshire Evening Post 1973, 2002
Leeds Mercury 1916
Yorkshire Evening Press 1916
Pontefract & Castleford Express 1916
Notes from Anne Batchelor

York Minster

21

Bomb Disposal Disaster

Snaith

1943

There was considerable debate about who should be responsible for ridding the country of unexploded bombs but at least there was agreement that it should be a military responsibility. Initially the task was shared between the RAF and the Army depending on where the bomb landed but by 1940 the job was plonked firmly in the lap of the RAF who formed special Bomb Disposal Flights and instituted six-week training courses in the task.

In April 1943 the organisation was changed again, this time into Flights which each contained a number of Squadrons. One such squadron was 5131 (BD) Squadron Commanded by Squadron Leader H H Apted. He was based at an airfield on the outskirts of Pollington, a little village near Goole but the Flight was known as Snaith so it would not be confused with a similar airfield outside Pocklington. The flights consisted of:

6205 Flt Snaith Yorkshire
6206 Snaith Yorkshire
6207 Morpeth
6208 Sealand Chester
6209 Thornaby Yorkshire

Their Operation Record Book shows that during the early part of June 1943 they had safely collected and disposed of bombs from all over the north of England so it was a shock when on 19 June the entry read:

'At 13.20 hours a serious explosion took place at the Bomb Dump RAF Station Snaith. Owing to the presence of exploding bombs and long delay action bombs full examination of damage and the removal of the bodies of eighteen missing airmen has not been possible. Group Captain Gray (CO

RAF Snaith) issued an operation order to the effect that the rendering safe of fused bombs in the bomb dump and the examination of all other bombs in the dump would be carried out under the personal direction of W/Cmdr Rowlands (Air Ministry O.10) and S/Ldr Apted (5131 (BD) Squadron) at 09.00 hours on 26 June 1943.'

A look around the area showed many bodies but no survivors so it had been decided to wait until it was deemed safe to go nearer. No one knew exactly how many bombs were involved, nor exactly what they were but it was believed that there were more than fifty bombs, many of them fused and ready for loading to aircraft. But work had to go on. Other airmen continued their vital work of making bombs safe and attending a British aircraft at Heslington which had crashed with nine bombs on board, whilst on the 20 June, Wing Commander Rowlands, who had been visiting the nearby RAF Sealand in Cheshire when the explosion occurred and had immediately gone to help, surveyed the scene at the bomb dump and awaited the time when it was deemed 'safe' to go into the area. On 26 June 'operations commenced' under the control of Rowlands, Flight Lieutenant Wilson of the Air Ministry and Squadron Leader H H Apted from the Snaith station, the harrowing task

War graves at Selby Cemetery

began of making the area safe so that the missing airmen could be found, identified and the bodies removed for burial. It took a great deal of courage from the three men to work there but by 30 June the task was complete.

The explosion was so horrific that the bodies of eight of the airmen were never found. Ten were buried in the War Graves Plot at Selby Cemetery but only nine could be identified. The remaining nine are commemorated on the RAF memorial at Runnymede, which honours over twenty thousand air personnel who have no known graves.

The victims were:
LAC – Leading Aircraftman
F/SGT – Flight Sergeant
AC2 – Aircraftman 2nd Class
AC1 – Aircraftman 1st Class

LAC H Bannatyne, Service No 1374377, thirty-five, son of Hugh and Jeannie Bannatyne, of Lanarkshire.

LAC Stephan Blackwell, Service No 1278728.

AC2 John Brown, Service No 1645687, thirty, son of John Joseph and Eleanor Brown.

LAC Hugh Finlayson, Service No 1374446, husband of Helen P Finlayson, of Edinburgh.

AC1 Oliver Richard Edward Dormon, Service No 1391523, twenty-two, son of Oliver.

Charles and Ethel Beatrice Dormon; husband of L G Dormon, of Holloway, London.

LAC Kenneth William Harris, Service No 1099749, twenty-two, son of Harold William and Mabel Harris, of Nottingham; husband of Dorothy May Harris, of Nottingham.

LAC Alfred Irvine, Service No 1374412, thirty-five, son of John and Jane Irvine, of Maybole, Ayrshire.

LAC John Jamieson, Service No 1374372, thirty-six, son of Grace Jamieson; husband of Agnes C Jamieson.

LAC James Roberton, Service No 1374376, thirty-seven, son of Thomas and Caroline. Lothian Roberton; husband of Helen Ann McKay Hope Roberton, of Edinburgh.

All the above are commemorated at Runnymede on Panel 171.

The following airmen were buried in Selby Cemetery War Graves Plot, though not all were able to be named on their gravestones:

F/Sgt Victor Harold Benfield, Service No 550323, twenty-four, son of Thomas Alfred. and Dorothy Sarah Benfield, of Shrivenham, Wiltshire, Grave 5318.

AC2 Joseph Ridley Cousin, Service No 1479455, Grave 5280.

Sgt Ernest David Francis, Service No 511509, thirty-one, son of Albert Charles David and Ellen Francis; husband of Kate Anne Francis, of Rhydyclafdy, Caernarvonshire. Grave No 5352.

AC2 Anthony Charles O'Donnell, Service No 1600881, son of George William and Margaret O'Donnell, of Brockenhurst, Hampshire. Grave No 5278.

AC2 Joseph Edward Powell, Service No 1419217, thirty-two, son of Edward and Mary Anne Powell; husband of Margaret Gertrude Powell, of Coton Hill, Shrewsbury, Shropshire. Grave No 5242.

LAC Herbert Rudge, Service No 1011171, twenty-three, son of Levie and Agnes Rudge, of Stoke-on-Trent; husband of Dorothy Rudge, of Fenton, Stoke-on-Trent, grave no 5282.

LAC Hugh Smith Service No 1374424. Grave no 5314.

AC1 Sidney Miller Stubbs, Service No 1312076, thirty-five, son of Herbert Percy and Edith Henderson Stubbs, of Newcastle-on-Tyne; husband of

Bomb Disposal memorial, Eden Camp

Bomb Disposal memorial detail

Mollie Stubbs. Grave No 5316.

LAC Robert Menzies Taylor, Service No 1374432, thirty-five, son of Alexander Dunn Taylor and Margaret Catto Taylor, of Aberdeen; husband of Beatrice Taylor, of Aberdeen. Grave No 5244.

Wing Commander Rowlands continued his work with bomb disposal and in July 1945 was invested with the George Cross by King George VI at Buckingham Palace. His citation reads:

'For over two years, Wing Commander Rowlands has been employed on bomb-disposal duties and has repeatedly displayed the most conspicuous courage and unselfish devotion to duty in circumstances of great personal danger.'

Air Marshal Sir John Rowlands died on Sunday 4 June 2006, aged ninety. There is now a memorial to the men of Bomb Disposal units at Eden Camp museum in North Yorkshire.

Sources:
Air Historical Branch (RAF) Ministry of Defence
http://www.cwgc.org – Commonwealth War Graves Commission website
Operations Record Book – RAF Snaith

Snaith Pollington Airfield

Index